THE ZOBRIST FAMILY:

LOOK WHAT GOD CAN DO

—BY TOM ZOBRIST—

WITH BILL BUTTERWORTH

The nonfiction imprint of
Tyndale House Publishers, Inc.

This book isn't really about Ben Zobrist and baseball. This book is about a family and their relationships with God. If you have questions and decisions to make in life, and you are ready for a closer relationship with God, this is a must-read book.
—Craig Gerdes, BEN'S MIDDLE SCHOOL COACH,
RETIRED EUREKA SCHOOL TEACHER

Tom Zobrist, my friend in ministry and life for over 30 years, is a blessed man. He has raised five children who walk with the Lord, has been married to his high-school sweetheart for over 40 years, has pastored for almost three decades a solid, vibrant, and Christ-honoring church, and much more. The book records highlights from Tom's life and some of the story concerning his most well-known son, Ben. Baseball fans will enjoy this behind-the-scenes look, and hopefully all readers will recognize the Lord's hand at every turn in the Zobrist family.
—Gary Gilley, SENIOR PASTOR OF SOUTHERN VIEW CHAPEL IN
SPRINGFIELD, ILLINOIS, AUTHOR AND SPEAKER

A fun and inspirational behind-the-scenes read on how a young couple from central Illinois raised a family that would produce the player who helped end a 108-year championship drought and become World Series MVP. Look what God can do! Immeasurably more than we ask or imagine.
—Kurt Pegler, WMBD-TV SPORTS DIRECTOR

This is a heartwarming, inspirational book about a man's devotion to his family and even more his zeal in serving the Lord, leading and living God's way. Whether you're a sports fan or not, you will enjoy reading it. —Tim Johnson, VP OF FIELD MINISTRY,
FCA MIDWEST REGION

Tom Zobrist has a powerful life changing message to share. His humor and "matter of fact" approach disarms you as he talks about the importance of family and the joys and failures of being a Christian as a son, husband, and dad. Tom writes, "...that when we desire God's will, he changes our hearts to want what He wants for us. When we pray, God changes us!" God's dreams for our lives are bigger, deeper and richer than our own.
—Tom Bennett, ILLINOIS STATE REPRESENTATIVE, DISTRICT 106

THE ZOBRIST FAMILY:
LOOK WHAT GOD CAN DO

—BY TOM ZOBRIST—

WITH BILL BUTTERWORTH

The nonfiction imprint of
Tyndale House Publishers, Inc.

Visit Tyndale online at www.tyndale.com.

Visit Tyndale Momentum online at www.tyndalemomentum.com.

TYNDALE, *Tyndale Momentum*, and Tyndale's quill logo are registered trademarks of Tyndale House Publishers, Inc. The Tyndale Momentum logo is a trademark of Tyndale House Publishers, Inc. Tyndale Momentum is the nonfiction imprint of Tyndale House Publishers, Inc., Carol Stream, Illinois.

The Zobrist Family: Look What God Can Do

Previously published in 2017 as *The Zobrist Family: Look What God Can Do* under ISBN 978-0-9994240-0-1.

First printing by Tyndale House Publishers, Inc., in 2018.

Designed by Converse Marketing, Peoria, Illinois; www.conversemarketing.com

ISBN 978-1-4964-3411-1

Printed in the United States of America

24	23	22	21	20	19	18
7	6	5	4	3	2	1

TABLE OF CONTENTS

DEDICATION

To Cindi and all our children
and grandchildren and...

When my Dad first told me he was approached to write a book about parenting me and his experience through the World Series, I was extremely skeptical. Don't get me wrong, my Dad has tons of wisdom to impart to everyone through his experiences; but I personally did not want to be the subject of conversation in this book, and I absolutely did not want people to put our family on a pedestal because of winning the World Series.

I knew Dad was enjoying being a parent of the World Series MVP and was taking speaking gigs as a result, but I was cautiously reminding him that the message better not be "Look what we did." After reading it, I am happy to say that this book reflects a much more appropriate message of humility and perspective through the story. *Look What God Can Do* is a great title, because it puts the focus back on faith in God's sovereign plan for our lives rather than our own grit and determination.

You'll see that my Dad did try—sometimes admittedly too hard—to teach me toughness and determination, but above all of that was a belief in walking with and trusting the God who can do anything. God works despite our best efforts and failures. He always knows best and always has a plan for our lives.

Personally, it is great to have my Dad's thoughts about some of these key events in my life. I know I speak for all of us kids that when your parents put down their important thoughts on a page, its something you want to keep for life. I've been given the blessing that a lot of people haven't—a Mom and Dad who loved me and wanted God's best for me. For that I will forever be grateful to both of them.

As I have a young family of my own, I want this desperately for my own children, and I am overjoyed that they already have this in their grandparents. All that to say, my Dad isn't just blowing smoke with these stories.

He doesn't make things up.

He's a pretty simple guy.

He loves God.

He loves the Word.

He loves people.

In these pages, you will find a simple and candid expression of a parent who is grateful for what God can do in his own life and the life of his family. Thanks for sharing this with us, Dad.

I love you Pops.
Ben Zobrist

This book is not a parenting book.

The last thing I want to do in writing this book is come off sounding like Cindi and I are the perfect parents or that we have it all together. People have asked us how to "raise an MVP" or what they can do to make sure their kids can be successful in baseball—or any sport, for that matter. Our answer is always the same: Don't channel your plans through your child, but help them find God's will and then help them follow that path. When we do that, God can do amazing things! That's what I want to be clear in these pages. This book is about what God has done in our family's life. It's about what God can do when we let Him work—and sometimes even when we don't.

All parents are going to make lots of mistakes, as will their kids. One of the amazing things that God does is that He continues to love us through all our blunders. His grace and love are not conditional, but are offered freely if we would receive it. He forgives, restores and then directs us to the path on which He wants us to walk. Our responsibility is to stay moldable through that process.

> *Second Timothy 3:16-17 says, "All Scripture is given by inspiration of God, and is profitable for doctrine, for reproof, for correction, for instruction in righteousness, that the man of God may be complete, thoroughly equipped for every good work."*

I think it was Warren Wiersbe who I first heard say that the four benefits of the Bible in these verses indicate that the Bible shows us what is right, what is wrong, how to get right, and how to stay right.

I remember hearing a famous Christian author say something like, "Wouldn't it be wonderful if children came with an instruction manual?" They did! It's called the Bible! There is so much written in God's Word concerning raising kids, marriage, setting a proper example, discipline, etc. When we pour ourselves into learning and living the Scriptures, the rough roads of child-rearing and marriage can be smoothed considerably. As you read this book, there will be a few passages presented that can help you in your walk with Jesus and maybe even in your parenting. This is not all of them, so I would encourage you to make Bible reading and study a daily practice and then take note of all that is there on parenting and marriage. Particularly in the book of Proverbs. It is loaded with practical advice on all the topics we are discussing. As you learn and maybe even feel convicted, remember that God loves you and is quick to forgive when we admit we have sinned.

First John 1:9 says, "If we confess our sins, He is faithful and just to forgive us our sins and to cleanse us from all unrighteousness." If God does this for us, then we in the family should do so for one another. We forgive and love one another no matter what. Our love is not conditional, just as God's love for us is not.

Our kids will tell you that our parenting style changed with our younger kids. There's a reason for that: We made mistakes and then made adjustments along the way. That's okay! That's called growth and God working in your life. Don't be too proud to admit when you are wrong and need to make an adjustment. Your kids will see your humility and learn to be humble from your example.

One last thing before we begin. Sometimes we as Americans think bigger is better; more influence is better than little influence. That's just not true. Your service to God is not about how big and how famous you are, but about how faithful you are. Is Ben's service for God better that mine because he is more famous or influences more people or has more opportunities? Or is mine just as important in a small church in a small town? I would argue that if one is where they are supposed to be in God's plan and they are faithful, that's all that matters. Be faithful to what God has called you to do! Whether you influence many or few, be faithful to what God calls you to each day. That is important. And when you do, "Look what God can do."

U.S. House of Representatives
Congressional Record

Representative Darin LaHood

November 15, 2016

APPLAUDING 2016 WORLD SERIES CHAMPIONS, THE CHICAGO CUBS

Mr. Speaker, I rise today to applaud the 2016 World Series champions, the Chicago Cubs, and to congratulate back-to-back World Series MVP, Ben Zobrist.

As the switch-hitting, utility player for the Cubs, Zobrist played a crucial role in bringing his team to victory.

At the top of the 10th inning in Game 7 of the World Series, Zobrist roped an RBI double giving the Cubs the decisive run in the 8-7 victory that won their team its first World Series championship since 1908.

Ben Zobrist is a native of Eureka, Illinois, located in my congressional district. The four-sport Eureka High School athlete went on to play baseball at Dallas Baptist University before launching his major league career.

More admirable than his talent is his character. In Major League Baseball, Zobrist has represented the sport with true Midwestern values. Ben is both a devout man of faith and a family man devoted to his wife and three children.

Ben Zobrist's commitment to God, family, and baseball make him not just a hero for his hometown of Eureka, Illinois, but a man that all of America can respect and admire.

CHAPTER ONE:

THE NATIONAL PRAYER BREAKFAST

The air was cold like the icy white marble buildings that February morning in Washington D.C., but my heart was warm like a seat by a crackling fire. It was a warmer day than usual for that time of year in D.C., but the morning chill was still in the air. My wife Cindi and I were in the Nation's capital to attend the National Prayer Breakfast at the Washington Hilton. This event was a big deal all by itself, but it was one of this year's participants that brought the warmth to my heart.

My son, Ben, was going to offer the opening prayer.

Can you imagine what it felt like inside of me to know that the little guy I had watched grow up was now a strong young man who would be part of one of the most significant events bringing the world of government and the world of our faith together in this annual gathering?

Cindi and I learned that Ben's wife, Julianna—an accomplished Christian singer—had been contacted by members of the National Prayer Breakfast Committee asking her to sing, and for Ben to participate in the event.

We also learned that our Congressman, Darin LaHood, and his father, former Secretary of Transportation Ray LaHood, had arranged for us not only to attend, but to be seated in the center of this gorgeous room and watch our son Ben deliver the opening prayer.

My sister, Linda Zobrist Morton, and her husband Bill got wind of what was going on and began making plans to attend the Breakfast on Thursday, February 2, 2017. Once we were made aware of it, they graciously arranged for us to accompany them to this amazing event.

That Thursday I was up early, showered, shaved, and dressed in my best suit and tie. By the way, the import of the event was magnified by the fact that we almost didn't get in! We had left Cindi's ID at the hotel and so I had to run back to our hotel a mile away and get it so that she could gain entrance. Nothing was going to keep us from being a part of this major event. We made our way to the Grand Ballroom, where the Breakfast was to take place. Large tables of ten were exquisitely set with china, crystal and linen.

I was blown away by the experience. The round tables were surrounded by men and women from all branches of government, as well as strong representation from the military. Since Cindi's father was a retired Brigadier General in the Air National Guard, seeing the many Christians in the military and their excitement about being a part of this special day especially gratified us.

I gazed up from my seat to find some recognizable faces at the head table. Along with several well-known politicians, there was Mark Burnett, the television producer responsible for such shows as *Survivor, The Apprentice,* and *Celebrity Apprentice,* seated right next to President Trump. And just a short distance away sat my son and daughter-in-law, Ben and Julianna. To see them surrounded by these government officials filled me with joy.

The last subject I want to get into is politics but I will say this much—Washington DC is not as bad as the media makes it out to be. I came away from this experience greatly encouraged about what the Lord is doing in our Nation's capital.

That, of course, was magnified by the fact that President Trump chose to attend the breakfast and even chose to offer some remarks. Here's a glimpse at a part of his speech:

> But most importantly, today I want to thank the American people. Your faith and prayers have sustained me and inspired me through some very, very tough times. All around America, I have met

amazing people whose words of worship and encouragement have been a constant source of strength.

What I hear most often as I travel the country are five words that never, ever fail to touch my heart, that's "I am praying for you." I hear it so often, "I am praying for you, Mr. President."

I was quite impressed by that part of his message—five words that never fail to touch his heart. That was good to hear. Later in the speech he emphasized the following thoughts about the place faith has had in the history of our great nation:

And America will thrive, as long as we continue to have faith in each other and faith in God. That faith in God has inspired men and women to sacrifice for the needy, to deploy to wars overseas and to lock arms at home, to ensure equal rights for every man, woman and child in our land. It's that faith that sent the pilgrims across the oceans, the pioneers across the plains and the young people all across America, to chase their dreams. They are chasing their dreams. We are going to bring those dreams back.

As long as we have God, we are never, ever alone. Whether it's the soldier on the night watch, or the single parent on the night shift, God will always give us solace and strength, and comfort. We need to carry on and to keep carrying on.

For us here in Washington, we must never, ever stop asking God for the wisdom to serve the public, according to His will.

For most people, hearing the President offer those remarks was certainly considered the high point of the morning. But not for me. For me, the highlight occurred much earlier in the program. As we took our assigned seats, the program was about to begin.

First, Senator Chris Coons from Delaware called us to order, followed by Senator John Boozman of Arkansas, who announced, "Ladies and Gentlemen, to offer our opening prayer, the Most Valuable Player of the 2016 World Series for the World Champion Chicago Cubs, Mr. Ben Zobrist!"

It was a surreal moment, watching that handsome young man walk to the lectern to deliver his prayer. The little boy I watched grow up, back then dressed mostly in jeans and t-shirts, was now this man. I watched as he pulled his notes from his perfectly tailored suit coat. He smiled and began in a confident voice:

> Thank you, Senator Coons, Senator Boozman. Let's go before the God who can not only end a 108-year drought—right?—but can do much much more.

The crowd beamed as he made his reference to the longstanding lack of a World Series championship for the Chicago Cubs. Then we all closed our eyes as he led us in prayer.

> Dear Gracious Heavenly Father, we come before You in this place with thankfulness in our hearts. We praise You and we want to acknowledge Your mighty power and amazing grace to allow us to come before You, O Holy God.

> Lord, You know that all I did was just hit a leather ball with a wooden stick and millions of people went nuts. But something much, much, more is happening here. As we pray to You, the Creator, Sustainer, and Redeemer of the world, draw near and listen to our hearts.

> I echo the book of Deuteronomy in saying, 'For I will proclaim the name of the Lord. Ascribe greatness to our God, the Rock. Your work is perfect, for all Your ways are justice. A God of faithfulness and without sin, just and upright are You.'

> I confess that many times we fail to acknowledge Your glory among our many accomplishments. Yet I pray today that You would remind us once again of Your power to heal, power to protect, power to liberate and ultimately, Your power to love, that will carry us forward as a nation.

> Please give our leaders wisdom and conviction to carry out Your good will in our country.

> We thank You for those courageous patriots who have given their lives and are giving them at this very moment to allow us the

freedom to meet here today and to have differing faiths and beliefs in our country.

Thank You for the many nations, lands, and faiths represented among us today that have all come together for a conversation this morning about the life and teachings of Jesus.

Let this be a morning of rejoicing in Your good grace and truth, Father, and let the Spirit of God fill this place to bring unity to our hearts under the banner of peace.

Bless this food we're about to partake in together and the words of our speakers today, and may everything that is said be to Your glory. I pray in the name of Your Son, Jesus Christ. Amen.

Once finished, he calmly walked back to his seat at the head table next to Julianna. My mind was flooded with thoughts of gratitude to the Lord. I thought about how grateful I was for this son of mine. But my mind continued to travel back even beyond that. I thought about how grateful I was that I came to a personal relationship with Jesus all those years ago. I thought about how grateful I was to meet and marry Cindi, my partner through all these years. I remembered the day Ben was born and how he grew up playing whiffle ball on a field we carved out of our backyard. I recalled his college baseball career and his moving up to the professional level. I felt a chill run down my spine when I realized yet again I had a son who played in three different World Series with three different ball clubs. That first World Series was in 2008, when he was with the Tampa Bay Rays. As a gift, Ben gave me a large color photo of him catching a fly ball in the outfield directly in front of the World Series logo on the right field wall. He inscribed it for me with these words:

From the Backyard to the World Series!
Look what God can do!
Your son, Ben Zobrist

Watching my son seated only a short distance from the President of the United States, I also thought of the wisdom of King Solomon, recorded in the Old Testament book of Proverbs:

Do you see a man who excels in his work?
He will stand before kings;

He will not stand before unknown men
–Proverbs 22:29

"All I did was just hit a leather ball with a wooden stick," he humbly declared. That single line kept repeating itself in my brain. "All I did was just hit a leather ball with a wooden stick." And as a result, the Lord blessed him, and now my son was opening the National Prayer Breakfast.

It was just about that time that the thought hit me:

God can do amazing things if we let Him work and just get out of the way.

And that's what this book is all about. Look what God can do, if we just let Him. Part of the reason that truth is so important to me is that for so many years and in so many ways, I have resisted it. Without realizing it, I've been telling God that His way is just fine, as long as it coincides with things that are under my control. When things go differently than I expected, or when things happen that are beyond my control, I get nervous, or fearful, or even angry.

Because my son is the MVP of the 2016 World Series and is not ashamed of his faith, I get a lot more credit for my parenting than I deserve. Perhaps this book will help to set the record straight. I'm human, just like you. I've done some things right and I've done plenty of things wrong. I want to share some lessons I've learned through some of those past joys and some of the painful mistakes I have made in my life.

Joys? I've had plenty. Mistakes? Many, as well. Let's start out with a doozy of a blunder...I thought I was a Christian because I grew up going to church.

CHAPTER TWO:

NINE DAYS THAT CHANGED MY LIFE

A new friend of mine recently visited me for a few days in my hometown of Eureka, Illinois. It's a tiny little town, but it's been my home for a long time and I just love it. I drove my friend over the country roads cut through the rolling hills to another nearby village called Morton, Illinois, where most of my extended family lives. It was a Saturday night and the weather was exceptionally fine—clear and comfortable. Eventually we ended up at the main hangout of our youth—the Dairy Queen in downtown Morton. Back in the old days the local movie theater was right across the street, so it was perfectly located for an after-movie treat. On this balmy Saturday night, a few dozen patrons had already gathered to enjoy their Blizzards, their dipped cones, and their Sundaes on the sidewalk in front of the D.Q.

I introduced my friend to just about everyone hanging around that night. I'm proud to be from a part of the country where people are kind and friendly, eager to shake your hand and offer you a smile. It didn't take long for my friend to utter the words I hear a lot in our part of the country. "Everyone I meet is either a Zobrist or married to a Zobrist!" he exclaimed. That's not exactly true, but it's pretty close.

The Zobrists go way back. Jakob Zobrist came to the United States in 1867 from his native Switzerland. My great-grandfather chose the town of Morton to begin his life of farming here in the states. His son Noah, had a son named Alpha, who was my dad.

Fast forward to March of 1976, when I was a senior at Morton High School. My friends and I frequently "loitered" in the halls of Morton High, near the cafeteria where there was lots happening. We were all looking forward to graduation, although I had no idea what I was going to do. At that point in my life, I really wasn't college material, and so I figured I could work for the family construction business like many Morton Zobrists. Little did I know, that idea was to change pretty radically and pretty quickly.

"Hey Tom, guess what," my buddy announced. "There is a recruiter from the United States Air Force on campus today."

I don't recall responding in any particular way, which perhaps bothered my friend.

"That's pretty cool," he pressed on, trying to get some sort of response from me, but I just nodded quietly. So, in a desperate attempt to get a rise out of me, he offered the ultimatum. "Tom," he said, "I *dare* you to go talk to the recruiter."

"You dare me?" I repeated back to him.

"Yep. You heard me. I betcha won't do it."

As an All-American boy, I was taught not to take dares lightly. So with firm resolve, I turned on my heels and proudly marched over to the table where the Air Force recruiter sat, his brochures piled high and his uniform gleaming.

I took the dare.

Before long, the recruiter had talked me into heading to St. Louis to sign up. And now you know how I ended up in the Air Force.

Looking back, I guess it was more than just reacting to the dare. I really was looking for some sort of new adventure and the promise offered by the Air Force would make that wish come true. They offered educational benefits, flying, and the chance to serve my country.

I signed up in St. Louis on Monday, March 15, 1976. Four days later, more big changes were in store—I had my first date with a delightful young lady named Cindi Cali. I guess you would describe it as a pretty typical first date—we went to dinner and a movie. I've heard other people talk about having a 'nice time' on a first date, but my evening with Cindi was much more than that. Don't ask me to explain it, but after that single date I just knew she was the girl I was going to marry and I told my mom so.

I was so positive about my future with Cindi that I immediately realized that if I had gone out with her before I had signed up for the Air Force, I would have never enlisted. I wasn't looking forward to being separated from her.

But God knew what He was doing, even though I second-guessed it at the time. "Lord, this is not the way I would have mapped it out," became a familiar refrain for control in my life, even after God blessed me with His grace time after time.

Even more change was in store. The following Monday night. Cindi got a phone call from Crystal, one of her girlfriends, and they talked about Jesus, as they had many times in the last year or so. Cindi heard the message of the simple Gospel—that Jesus died for the sins of the world, including hers, yours, and mine; and if we place our trust in Christ as our Personal Savior, we will be instantaneously born into the Family of God. The Holy Spirit will come and live within us during our days here on Earth, and we will have a home in Heaven when we die. She had chosen to reject this message before, but on this Monday night, March 22, 1976, she accepted the Lord as her Savior. Little did I know how much that decision would affect me.

The next day was Tuesday—nine days since I had signed up for the Air Force. Cindi found me and took me aside for a very serious conversation. "Something very important happened to me last night, Tom," she began. "I accepted Jesus as my Savior." I didn't understand what she was talking about. She continued to explain to me all that was said over the phone with her girlfriend Crystal. When she got to the end, she made her pronouncement.

"I want to serve Jesus with my life. So, Tom, if you don't want to do that, I don't want to date you anymore."

Now that's a jam-packed nine days!

Panicked at hearing Cindi's words, I declared myself to be a Christian. All my life I believed I was a Christian because I went to church and did everything they told me to do. I honestly believed that!

So, because I liked this girl so much, I began to attend Christian events with her, Crystal, and another friend of mine, Barney, who had become a believer and in whose life I had seen a change. I began to learn Bible verses like:

> *For by grace you have been saved through faith, and that not of yourselves, it is a gift from God, not of works, lest any man should boast. —Ephesians 2: 8-9*

Sure, I was raised in a home with strong Christian values, and it was a home where church attendance was important. But what I was learning, along with the Bible verses I was reading, made a very important concept perfectly clear:

You can go to church, and not be a Christian. You can know about Jesus but not know Jesus.

It was during one of these Christian "double dates" that we ended up at an outreach event featuring David Wilkerson, the author of the best-selling book *The Cross and the Switchblade*. David gave the plan of salvation in the same simple and clear way Cindi had explained it to me, and it was all I needed to hear. It was the first time I realized that I wasn't a Christian. I lived my life thinking I was, but wasn't! I told Cindi that I needed to do that. She took my hand and led me forward, and I received Christ that night.

So that was the moment I put my trust in Christ. That was the moment I was saved. It was the climax of those nine days that changed my life.

How about you, dear reader? Do you know the difference between going to church and becoming a child of God? The most famous verse in the Bible makes it perfectly clear:

For God so loved the world that He gave His only begotten Son that whosoever believeth in Him should not perish, but have everlasting life. —John 3:16

Have you accepted the Lord as your Personal Savior? You can do it right now in the quietness of your heart if you want to. The true God knows your thoughts and you can offer Him a silent prayer of confession of your sins and acceptance of His grace. Nothing would bring me greater joy than knowing you reached out to Him as a result of the sharing of my story. I urge you to do it right now.

Meanwhile, back in Morton, I was all signed up, ready to go into the Air Force. God hadn't made a mistake in allowing me to enlist the way I did at the time I did. Upon graduation from high school the next step was heading off to Basic Training in San Antonio, Texas, where the Lord had even more lessons for me to learn.

CHAPTER THREE:

THE AIR FORCE

"Send Airman Zobrist down here right away.
Someone is here to see him."

It was the voice of my First Sergeant blaring over the intercom in our barracks. I had not had anyone come to see me since I moved to San Antonio for Basic Training.

The thought of someone coming to see me was far from encouraging. Frankly, it frightened me, for I was certain it was someone with bad news. As I hustled down to meet my visitor at the front of the Base, I had become increasingly more convinced it was something tragic. By the time I got to my visitor, I was certain that my mother had died and I was called out to be informed of the painful truth.

As I approached, I discovered it was not a single visitor, but two of them. Both were men dressed in Air Force uniforms with the markings indicating that they were First Lieutenants. Now I was really worried.

"Is everything okay?" I blurted out.

"Yes Sir," the men responded kindly.

"What's going on here?" I quizzed, still completely in the dark. Their answer was one I had never expected.

"We're from a ministry known as the Navigators," one began. "We were contacted by your sister Linda back in Chicago. She's concerned that you may be all alone in your Christian faith, so we're here to let you know that we would love to be available to you, if you'd be interested."

Along with being greatly relieved that I wasn't receiving bad news, I was thrilled that my sister had been so thoughtful. Unknown to her, Cindi and I had prayed that God would provide some fellowship and He did! The first night I was there, the guy in the bunk next me told me he was a brand new believer when he saw me reading my Bible. He and I eventually started a prayer group around our beds that grew to a dozen

or more in the time we were there. But the Navigator fellowship was sweet as well, as those two lieutenants came and picked me up for fellowship a few times. More importantly, I saw the Christian world was small and that we are never really alone.

This was also my introduction to all that was being done by the Navigators globally, and especially with the military. Eventually I ended up at Carswell AFB in Fort Worth, Texas, where I became a Crew Chief on a B-52 bomber, learning how to maintain these behemoths while simultaneously learning how to share my faith. It was one of my friends, a co-pilot named Frank Christian, who said to me one night, "Hey Tom, there's a guy here on the Base who's starting a new ministry called the Navigators. He will teach us how to do evangelism in the dorms. Are you interested?"

I nodded my head in agreement, and soon we were off to meet Doug and Jan Sherman. I eagerly joined forces with them in their zeal for evangelism and discipleship. Doug was the perfect disciple for me since he was a real bulldog of a man. "We're going to go door to door in the dorm and try to lead guys to Christ," he announced. If I looked a little panicked, it didn't bother Doug in the least. "I'll take the first door and then Zobrist, you'll take the second one."

I remember meekly replying, "I'm not sure I can do that, Doug. It's kind of scary." Military dorms aren't the friendliest of places.

Doug had no time for sheepishness, so he replied to me immediately and directly. "Tom, you are going to have to make a decision, right here, right now," he urged. "Either you're going to be a fool in the eyes of God or a fool in the eyes of man. You decide."

So I did it.

And it was a good thing. It was harmless. Sure, there were some guys who said some unkind things, but I quickly learned from Doug that my job is to share my faith and in doing so, I'm planting seeds, even with those who appear uninterested or mean.

I am so very grateful that there were strong Christian men and women who were looking out for me in those early days of my walk with the Lord. Some were even hundreds of miles away, yet somehow they knew that I would need the encouragement that could come only from a brother or sister in Christ who would offer comfort, hope, and peace by sharing inspiring passages from the Word of God, the Bible.

One such couple was my sister and brother-in-law, Linda and Bill. Vividly I remember the day Bill sent me a note in the mail with two passages of Scripture written for me to read, reflect, and meditate.

I have never forgotten these powerful passages. The first was Psalm 1:1-6.

> ¹ Blessed is the man
> Who walks not in the counsel of the ungodly,
> Nor stands in the path of sinners,
> Nor sits in the seat of the scornful;
>
> ² But his delight is in the law of the Lord,
> And in His law he meditates day and night.
>
> ³ He shall be like a tree
> Planted by the rivers of water,
> That brings forth its fruit in its season,
> Whose leaf also shall not wither;
> And whatever he does shall prosper.
>
> ⁴ The ungodly are not so,
> But are like the chaff which the wind drives away.
>
> ⁵ Therefore the ungodly shall not stand in the judgment,
> Nor sinners in the congregation of the righteous.
>
> ⁶ For the Lord knows the way of the righteous,
> But the way of the ungodly shall perish.
> —Psalm 1:1-6

The other Scripture was also from the Old Testament..

> ⁸ This Book of the Law shall not depart from your mouth, but you shall meditate in it day and night, that you may observe to do according to all that is written in it. For then you will make your way prosperous, and then you will have good success. —Joshua 1:8

Thanks to Bill delivering those specific Scripture verses, I learned the importance of understanding and applying the principles of the Bible and using them to serve the Lord with all of my heart.

I was so blessed, not only to have long distance encouragers, but the guys on the Base that kept me on track. To this day, I can't thank God enough for the ministry of the Navigators.

This is all leading up to a very important principle here, so let me spell it out in clear fashion:

You become like the people you spend time with.

The Apostle Paul communicated it clearly and simply in his first letter to the Corinthians:

> *Do not be deceived; Bad company corrupts good morals.*
> *—First Corinthians 15:33*

Make no mistake, I was far from an angel growing up. As a teenager especially, I liked to party and I must confess at that time in my life I would drink to drunkenness. Why did I do that? Friends with whom I was hanging out encouraged me to do this, but I can't blame them. It was my own sinful desire to be accepted any way I could that led to that end. By contrast, the joy of the Christian brothers and sisters that God brought in my life cannot be underestimated.

King Solomon discussed the powerful impact friends have on one another in the first chapter of the book of Proverbs:

> [10] *My son, if sinners entice you,*
> *Do not consent.*
>
> [11] *If they say, "Come with us,*
> *Let us lie in wait to shed blood;*
> *Let us lurk secretly for the innocent without cause;*
>
> [12] *Let us swallow them alive like Sheol, [a]*
> *And whole, like those who go down to the Pit;*
>
> [13] *We shall find all kinds of precious possessions,*
> *We shall fill our houses with spoil;*
>
> [14] *Cast in your lot among us,*
> *Let us all have one purse"—*
>
> [15] *My son, do not walk in the way with them,*
> *Keep your foot from their path;*

¹⁶ For their feet run to evil,
And they make haste to shed blood.

¹⁷ Surely, in vain the net is spread
In the sight of any bird;

¹⁸ But they lie in wait for their own blood,
They lurk secretly for their own lives.

¹⁹ So are the ways of everyone who is greedy for gain;
It takes away the life of its owners.
—Proverbs 1: 10-19

As you read those verses, can you feel the powerful pull a friend can have? The bad news is that's the power of a 'sinner enticing' you. Call it peer pressure or people-pleasing or whatever you want, those around us can draw us into situations and behaviors that are sinful. But the other side of that same coin offers good news—good friends, godly friends, those who share your same values and beliefs can produce the same kind of power, except that it's power for good, not evil. God uses the people in our lives to teach us through their influence. The Holy Spirit taught me many things through my friends back in those Air Force days. And He continues to use friends to this day.

Having said all that concerning the power of friends, there is one other aspect of life that is even more powerful—and that's family. A year and half into my Air Force days, it was time for me to get married and start having some children, adding even more to the already large Zobrist population.

CHAPTER FOUR:

NEWLYWEDS

I continued my relationship with Cindi, even though we were hundreds of miles apart. With me in the Air Force stationed in Texas, and Cindi back home in Illinois, it was less than an ideal situation.

The truth is that in the year leading up to our wedding, I had only seen her a couple of times. We were approaching marriage with absolutely no pre-marital counseling or any other kind of assistance in helping us make wise and mature decisions. I had been growing with the Navigators, but wasn't sure who or what was feeding my fiancée.

I firmly believed that the Lord had brought us together. That ended up being even more significant than one might think. The reason that was important is that, as I look back, that was the only thing the two of us had in common at that point in our lives.

We were married December 17, 1977, in an evening ceremony held at First Mennonite Church back in Morton, Illinois. Neither Cindi nor I attended there, but it was chosen for its size. It was large enough to contain the Zobrist family, since most of the Morton Zobrists would be attending.

We were quite a couple, Cindi and me; young and innocent and immature. Cindi turned 19 just seven weeks before, and I turned 20 just three weeks before. Looking back, I can't believe that our parents approved! I guess the phone bills proved to be too much for them to handle month-to-month. That was back before free cell phone long distance. I remember Andy, Cindi's dad, telling me that normally he didn't think two could live cheaper than one; but in our case, we could without hours of long distance calls each month.

I remember walking my mother down the aisle to her front row pew, and all the time I was doing that, I was so light-headed and nauseous that I was certain I was going to pass out. I don't remember a great deal about the actual ceremony. I do remember my nephew Nathan was ringbearer and was carrying the actual rings. We rehearsed moving from the groom's side to the bride's the night before with no problem, but we failed to factor in the train of Cindi's wedding dress. When the ring ceremony began, as Nathan moved from one side to the other, he encountered the train and astutely improvised in this unforeseen circumstance. Nathan, just having turned 4 a couple of months before, standing broad jumped across the train and landed on it. I can still see Cindi's head jerking back like a rag doll with a bad case of whiplash. We still laugh about it today.

The rest of the ceremony went off without a hitch, and the reception was lovely as well. We were so grateful for all the family and friends that made the effort to attend the event that, naturally, we were the last ones to leave the reception. And since it was an evening wedding, that means we didn't get to our hotel room till after 1 AM. To make matters worse, we had an 8 AM flight the following morning. As a result, our wedding night was much different than most people would think.

Early in the morning, as Cindi slept, I watched her quietly beside me. I couldn't help but be thankful for what God had done, but I found myself plagued with a couple of reoccurring questions:

Who is that?

And what have I done to her life?

She was 19 years old. We were both young and immature and didn't really know one another. We definitely needed some help. But we didn't get any right away. The next morning we were up and on our way to an Alabama beach house that had been provided to us through the kindness of my Uncle Noah (you'll read more about him in a later chapter). Our honeymoon proved to be rocky. We were mistaken to be brother and sister on an outing at the resort, reminding us of our youth and immaturity. We fought several times and both wondered if we had made the biggest mistake of our lives. But we were committed to the decision we had made and stuck with it. That's what we saw modeled in the family around us and we were going to follow those examples.

After Christmas and one week of marriage, it was time to head to Texas together. I was so excited to be taking my bride with me. I couldn't understand why she was weeping as we drove away from her parents' house. A few blocks away, she realized she forgot her purse. We turned around and went back. I walked in the house and saw her mom weeping and her dad consoling her. They had hidden their feelings from us earlier, but now I could see the pain this was causing them. I was confused and sad. Cindi cried herself to sleep that night in a hotel in Oklahoma City as we made our way south. Finally in our little apartment in Fort Worth, things didn't get easier.

We needed to grow together, both physically and spiritually, but at the time we were ignorant of how to proceed. And it just got worse. When I returned to my base, my plane was put on alert for several months causing me to have to be away several days a week. I stopped fellowshipping with the Navigators and we stopped going to church. Both were painfully unwise decisions. The very spiritual nourishment we needed, I was starving us from. So, not surprisingly, after only two months of marital life, Cindi wanted to go home. Looking back, I can't blame her. We were young and dumb and we needed to get help.

Cindi called her father to tell him of her decision to come home. She was met by a firm sounding voice on the other end of the line. "Put Tom on the phone," he insisted in strong tones. Cindi handed me the phone, which I put up to my ear. His first comment floored me.

"Tom, you married her, you need to keep her," he stated in unequivocal terms. "Work out your problems." Andy retired from the Air National Guard as a Brigadier General. At the time, he was a Lieutenant Colonel and I was an Airman First Class. I said, "Yes Sir!" And the phone call had ended.

I am so grateful to Cindi's dad for the counsel he gave on that phone call. It was as if he forced us to grow up. In our immaturity, we had fallen away from our spiritual lives a bit, so I got re-plugged into the local Navigators ministry by beginning to attend a couple's Bible study and also began attending church again. The counseling we should have received before marriage, we received after. Better late than never, right? It was not the last trial our marriage would have to endure, but we were being equipped with what we needed to survive.

So, these days, since I am a Pastor of a church, I perform my fair share of weddings. I always insist on several pre-marital counseling sessions and I usually begin by saying to the engaged couple, "What I will tell you is what I wish they had told me!"

I assign them a book to read, *Preparing for Marriage God's Way* by Wayne Mack. The book is a gold mine of information for those getting ready to be man and wife. Some of the topics discussed in the book are:

- Real Love

- God's Blueprint for Marriage

- Your Most Important Relationship

- Communicating

- Resolving Conflict

- Being a Husband

- Being a Wife

- Family Finances

- Sex as God Intended

- Your Special Day

And then he concludes the book with chapters concerning a Six Month Check-up and A One Year Check-up.

I'm thorough in my pre-marital counseling; but based on what Cindi and I went through, you can understand why.

One last issue I'm really big on—I always encourage those in pre-marital counseling to avoid the evening weddings and instead schedule an afternoon wedding. Our 1 AM debacle taught me the importance of that decision. After all, you have only one first night.

Because I believe so strongly in marriage, when I get to officiate a wedding ceremony, I make sure the bride and groom get one more dose of what the Scriptures teach regarding that subject. I always try to make it interesting and appropriate to the occasion.

As an example, here's a portion of a wedding ceremony that I performed recently. The ceremony was outside on a hot afternoon, thus explaining the context of what you are about to read:

> It's hard to stay cool when the weather is hot. These aren't the coolest of clothes. We joked the other day about wearing shorts and T-shirts today. In such a beautiful setting, surrounded by family and friends, you'll enjoy this day no matter what the weather. But what about staying cool when the heat and pressures of life are on? If you can apply the passage that you have chosen, you will be able to stay cool when life heats up. First, we wear COOL CLOTHES.
>
> *Colossians 3:12-14 says, "Therefore, as the elect of God, holy and beloved, put on tender mercies, kindness, humility, meekness, longsuffering; 13 bearing with one another, and forgiving one another, if anyone has a complaint against another; even as Christ forgave you, so you also must do. 14 But above all these things put on love, which is the bond of perfection."*
>
> The first element of wearing cool clothes is you must be "elect of God" having believed in Jesus. This helps one maintain control through hard times. Without God being part of your lives and home, these following traits will be hard to attain. And when we

are born again, we are made holy by the new birth and we go from being enemies of God to being beloved. We are accepted into the presence of a holy God. We now can live like Jesus. How does that look?

When the world says you have the right to get revenge, you can choose to show mercy and kindness. Be quick to forgive and slow to anger. Next, be humble. Arrogance and pride are not attractive. Humility is beautiful and will strengthen your marriage relationship. Jesus was the ultimate example of humility, while being God, did not demand what were His rights, but submitted to the cross so that we might live. He's our example.

Patience and forgiveness are on the list, too. Sometimes before we are married we think our future spouse is perfect. Soon we find out that it is not so. We learn patience and forgiveness or we will grow bitter and frustrated. Forgiveness protects us from the onslaughts of Satan as he tries to get you to offend one another, thus driving a wedge between you. You aren't perfect now and you never will be. We must forgive, over and over again. Jesus said up to 70x7 times. That's an unlimited amount.

Also remember that true love is selfless. It will hold you together when the storms of life come crushing in around you.

Here are some additional attitudes we need to put on to stay cool.

Colossians 3:15-17, "And let the peace of God rule in your hearts, to which also you were called in one body; and be thankful. 16 Let the word of Christ dwell in you richly in all wisdom, teaching and admonishing one another in psalms and hymns and spiritual songs, singing with grace in your hearts to the Lord. 17 And whatever you do in word or deed, do all in the name of the Lord Jesus, giving thanks to God the Father through Him."

Peace and thankfulness: Be content with what God gives you and realize that He is in control.

Phil. 4:6-7 says, "Be anxious for nothing, but in everything by prayer and supplication, with thanksgiving, let your requests be made known to God; and the peace of God which surpasses all understanding, will guard your hearts and minds through Christ Jesus."

We can't always have things our way. Some things are out of our control. To accept the things that are out of our control is to choose the peace of God. This helps us to be thankful.

Commit to a strong spiritual home: Reading the Bible, praying, attending church together, serving God together, all contribute to a strong spiritual home. All are necessary to keep you growing and thriving as a family and to set an example for your children, should the Lord bless you with them.

If in doubt, do what Jesus would do, all the while being thankful. If you can't see Jesus doing it, neither should you.

I call the second part of this passage THE COOL FAMILY.

Colossians 3:18-21 says, "Wives, submit to your own husbands, as is fitting in the Lord. ¹⁹ Husbands, love your wives and do not be bitter toward them. ²⁰ Children, obey your parents in all things, for this is well pleasing to the Lord. ²¹ Fathers, do not provoke your children, lest they become discouraged."

You will not be able to fulfill these verses if you don't first put on the "Cool Clothes" we talked about before.

Wives, submit to your husbands. This is not popular in today's culture, but it is fitting. It is what God designed. God's plans haven't changed, even though our world has and not always for the good of the family! Submission sounds like a horrible scenario, but if the husband is fulfilling his role it makes it easier. Unfortunately, men sometimes fail which makes this difficult to do. Not impossible though.

Secondly, Husbands, love your wives. We're talking about agape love, expressing unselfish esteem for the other. It's a love that always does what's best, no matter the circumstances. Remember John 3:16? Jesus is the supreme example. This type of love is a choice you make, not a feeling you have. You choose to do what is right and you will have the right feelings in time. Husbands love your wives, even when it isn't so easy.

Children are still to obey their parents, not demand their rights. Verse 21 qualifies this. Children will want to obey, if they are loved properly and disciplined properly. Fathers that are harsh, demanding, and demeaning can discourage their children and create unhealthy homes.

These are crazy concepts and expectations in today's world. There have been so many changes. But, along with the changes in the family today has come an increase in abuse, discontent, and broken homes. A return to Biblical standards would help. If you, as a couple, apply these in your home, you can avoid many of the pitfalls this world creates.

Soon we'll be inside enjoying the air conditioning and cooling off. But always remember, you can keep your family cool by putting on these attitudes that reflect Christ in your lives. When you do, you'll stay cool through any trial life throws your way and you will find the comfort and joy that you desire today.

Here you see Ben and Julianna just > five seats from President Trump at the National Prayer Breakfast.

< With Darin LaHood at the Capitol. Darin and his dad, Ray, were instrumental in getting us tickets for the National Prayer Breakfast.

∧ LEFT TO RIGHT: Bill Morton, Linda Morton, Julianna's mom Cheryl Gilmore, Ben and Julianna, Tom and Cindi

< Being an Air Force veteran, it was an honor to meet General Paul Selva, the Vice Chairman of the Joint Chiefs of Staff.

Cindi and Tom's wedding ∧

This was our family while ↗
I was in school in Kansas
City. LEFT TO RIGHT:
Cindi, Tom, Ben,
Serena, and Jessica

Ben, age 6 months >

Ben and I experienced his >
little league together as I
helped coach.

HERRY PARDEE PHOTOGRAPHY

< Andy and Dot Cali,
Cindi's parents, at
Ben's wedding in
2005.

∧ LEFT TO RIGHT: Cindi
holding Jessica, Ben's
great-grandpa Noah
Zobrist holding Ben,
and then me.

< LEFT TO RIGHT: Serena,
Tom, Cindi, Ben, Pete,
Jess, and Noah in 2001.

∧ My mom and dad. My dad married
the prettiest girl in town!

∧ LEFT TO RIGHT: Me, Uncle Noah, Cindi's
dad Andy "The General" Cali, and Ben

Ready for the World Series > at Wrigley. LEFT TO RIGHT: Jessica, Julianna, Julianna's parents Jeff and Cheryl Gilmore, Pete, Serena and her husband Michael, me, Cindi, Courtney, and Noah.

It felt like Chicago vs. > Everybody when the Cubs were down 3–1 in the World Series. This picture was taken after we won Game Seven. I think we look pretty good considering it was the middle of the night and we had celebrated on the field in the rain.

Uncle Noah with > Julianna and Cindi.

Christmas morning 2015. > Ben got everyone a Cubs jersey for Christmas.

< The World Series was stressful at times.

∨ Our kids, everyone but Ben and Julianna, at the World Series. LEFT TO RIGHT: Michael and Serena Grimm, Jessica and Robert Reeves, Courtney, Noah, and Pete.

∧ I never thought I'd be at this news conference.

Ben hugged ∧ Grandma Shirley, my mom, when Eureka had a rally for him after the Cubs won the World Series in 2016. My sister got her a seat in the front row. About 1,800 turned out for that celebration.

Okay . . . this was staged > before Game Seven, but it turned out to be prophetic!

2016 WORLD CHAMPIONS!

< Celebrating on Wrigley Field after winning the pennant!

< Noah warming me up outside of Wrigley Field on "First Pitch Night." All three of my boys had a part in that special night.

v Here we are on "First Pitch Night" with Ben's family. Cindi and me, Zion, Ben, Blaise, Julianna, and Kruse.

< My aunt Marilyn Zobrist Donahue lives in the Chicago area and is a gracious hostess to many of us when we are at Cubs games. Her husband, Dan Donahue, was a former owner of the Milwaukee and Atlanta Braves. He was an encouragement to Ben as his professional career was getting going. LEFT TO RIGHT: Me, Cindi, Julianna holding Blaise, Zion, Lucy, Kruse, Aunt Marilyn, and Serena (Lucy's mom).

CHAPTER FIVE:
SCHOOL DAYS

I got out of the Air Force in 1980 and immediately returned to Morton to go to work for Zobrist Construction Company. In a sense, it was a sort of rite of passage for a male Zobrist to invest some time in that company. As a matter of fact, every son of the company owners could buy a part of the company. That's one more example of the close-knit connection of the Zobrists.

It was a slow time in the construction business. The greater Peoria area was in a bit of a depression. Caterpillar, one of the biggest industries in the area, was laying off thousands of employees. Rather than laying me off, I was kept busy doing a variety of jobs not necessarily construction-related, since those were few and far between. I would do things like become the janitor in the Field Shopping Center that the company owned. I was just pleased to be working.

But the Lord was putting it in my heart that I should investigate furthering my education. As a military veteran, I had the old GI Bill, which would pay for my schooling. I could go to school, collect on the GI Bill, and the business would only have to pay me part time. It was a win-win. So in January of 1982, I enrolled in the local Junior College, Illinois Central College. I took General Education and business classes, particularly in the area of data processing, thinking I might use it in the company work someday. Along with my schooling, my uncles kept me busy with 25 hours a week of work.

I did much better than I expected at school, since I didn't do that well in high school, academically. I learned how to study and actually enjoyed it. It's shocking what doing your homework can do! Looking back, I now see that these events were all used by God to prepare me for a future in ministry.

One day, I was golfing with one of the elders from the church I was attending, named Wilbur Miller (everyone called him Bud). He brought up a subject not golf-related. It would prove to be pivotal. "Tom," Bud said to me that day, "Did you know that I was on the Board of Calvary Bible College in Kansas City?"

"No, sir, I didn't know that," I admitted, not knowing why he would want me to be aware of that fact in the first place.

After a brief pause he continued, "You should consider going there."

"Me?" I replied in disbelief. "Why?"

"Tom, I believe you have real potential for ministry," was his candid evaluation of my potential.

Within a few months, another elder, Maynard Mathewson, my pastor Mike Boyle, and a few trusted friends all encouraged me to go to Bible College and prepare for some sort of ministry. The seed was firmly planted in my heart, but acting on it took a little more time.

Instead of heeding the call and moving on to Bible College, I stayed on at ICC through the spring and fall of 1983. As I prepared to graduate from ICC in December of 1983 with an Associates Degree, I was looking forward to getting a Bachelors degree in another eighteen months.

It was during that fall semester that I took a drive to the local university where I intended to finish my degree, in order to pay a visit to my guidance counselor. It was also during that time that I realized my heart was changing. It started with an increasingly uncomfortable feeling whenever I walked through the halls of the school's campus. I even mentioned that to Cindi when she was with me. It was to reach its apex that October evening.

To kick things off, on this particular Friday I was issued a $25 parking ticket in one of the parking lots of the college. I was furious. It had been a terrible week and now this! Fortunately, Friday night was the beginning of the Missions Conference at our church, so I went there that evening and enjoyed the teaching and the fellowship, even though my attitude was a little sour.

The next morning there was a Men's Breakfast that featured a speaker named Dr. Al Platt, who was President of Central American Mission. As he rose to present his message, he opened his Bible to Exodus, where he began to preach the familiar story of Moses and the Burning Bush. To this day I don't know exactly what he said that had such impact, but I can describe it best this way...

...that was my moment.

God got ahold of me. It was as if Dr. Platt was speaking directly to me and telling me that I was avoiding God's call, much as Moses had. I had to get up from my seat and walk out of the room. Mike Boyle saw what was happening and followed me out.

"Tom, are you okay?" Mike asked with genuine compassion.

I looked him squarely in the eyes and told him what the Lord was laying on my heart. "I think I need to go to Bible School," was how I phrased it to him.

Mike smiled and responded, "Yeah, you do."

Now I was smiling. Mike and I had talked about me going into fulltime ministry for years and now it finally appeared that I was getting the message.

But what would Cindi think? This was going to be a big decision with lots of change as a result. We had three young children and there were no on-line classes. This was going to be another big move away from home. When I got home I sat her down and told her what had occurred at the Men's Breakfast.

She burst into tears.

Before I could do anything to console her, she blurted out, "I've been praying that you would make that decision for years!" I asked why she didn't tell me. She said it had to be my decision. And she was right.

So we were headed off to Bible school.

My initial plan was to enroll in Dallas Theological Seminary, like my pastor had. I would finish my Bachelor's Degree at Dallas Bible College and then begin at DTS.

But Bud wanted me to make a visit to Kansas City first, to check out Calvary Bible College. So to honor his request, Cindi and I made a trip out there in January of 1984. It was a cold winter's night when we pulled up to the entrance of the campus. As I looked at it, I kept rubbing my eyes, feeling like I had been in something like this before. It turns out I was correct. Calvary Bible College was in the middle of taking over an Air Force Base that was closing down! I was flashing back to my Air Force days as I entered the campus. It helped in those memories that there was still an Air Force guard attending the entrance. Cindi expressed her displeasure for the military environment, since she was never a big fan of the Air Force, having been in it most of her life through her dad and me. But, by the light of day, everything would change.

The next morning Bud had arranged for me to meet the President of the College, Leslie Madison. Dr. Madison, a Dallas Seminary graduate, had the distinction of being the first student to earn all A's at the seminary, as reported by Dr. John Walvoord, the Seminary's President at the time.

Dr. Madison and I got along well and had a very comfortable conversation. It was so comfortable that I pressed to ask him a question that had begun to develop in my mind. "Dr. Madison," I leaned in to inquire, "Do you think I need to go to Seminary?"

I'll never forget his response. "Tom, if we didn't prepare you well here at the College, we would go out of business!"

Point well taken.

Next, Bud set an appointment with Dr. J. Elwood Evans. A former member of the faculty at Dallas Theological Seminary (and Dr. Walvoord's brother-in-law), he still lived in Dallas, but flew to Kansas City each Monday afternoon, taught a full load of classes Tuesday through Thursday, and then flew back home Thursday afternoon. He did this for several years.

After conversing with Dr. Evans for a while, I once again brought up the subject of the necessity of Seminary. In his majestic manner, Dr. Evans responded by saying, "Tom, God may have a plan for you that doesn't include seminary, so you'd better prepare now! You have a wife and three children to think about."

"That's good counsel," I replied. Then I added, "I'm thinking that I may attend Dallas Bible College..."

Dr. Evans interrupted abruptly. "Now you listen to me, boy, Calvary Bible College is the best Bible College in the entire United States of America. Don't cheat your Bible education because you think you might go to seminary."

With that glowing endorsement from such a well-respected academic, I went back to our room and announced to Cindi that we were moving to Kansas City.

By the way, I have to share one more story on Dr. Evans. I did end up attending Calvary Bible College in Kansas City and as a result I sat under Dr. Evans for several of my classes. I turned in a paper one day of which I was especially proud. To my dismay, when it was returned to me, Dr. Evans had given me the grade of a B. I was shocked and disappointed so I decided to confront Dr. Evans about it. I visited him that evening in his makeshift "hotel room" in the school's administration building.

"Dr. Evans," I asked him, "why did you give me a B on that paper?"

"It was good work," was his reply.

"An A?" I pressed.

"Good work, Tom, not A work," was his pronouncement. What could I say? I received three B's while at Calvary and one of them was in his class. I'm thankful for teachers that pushed me to excellence and not to settle for anything but. That would prove helpful in ministry.

As that first visit to Calvary Bible College was coming to an end, Cindi and I could already see beyond the Air Force buildings and started seeing the people. We were excited.

My first semester at Calvary was the fall of 1984. I'm thankful that God used Bud Miller to get me there. He proved to be a constant blessing as every time he was on campus to attend a board meeting, he took me to breakfast or lunch and encouraged me to keep moving, even when I felt like quitting. He reminded me that if God led me there, God would get me through. Dr. Evans once talked me out of quitting as well. It was not easy with a family, but God was always faithful to provide what we needed just in time. I would end up taking 105 hours in three years (that's a lot) and graduated in May of 1987. It truly was a "Look what God can do!" experience!

Okay, so now I'm a Bible College graduate. What's next?

As I moved closer to graduation, I would hear different ministries introduced to us in Chapel and I would wonder if that particular ministry was the one that I would work with. To play it safe, I'd invite the Chapel speaker home to meet Cindi, so she could get a feel for the opportunities that were out there. I spanned the entire gamut of ministries, too. Cindi would be making dinner for a representative of an Inner City Mission one night and then a Foreign Mission Board executive the next. I was trying to cover all the bases.

I saw many of my classmates graduate from CBC and stay in secular jobs and I didn't want to fall into that trap. I wanted to serve the Lord in some capacity. I figured I would try my hand at church planting and start a church where one was needed. I was just about settled on joining forces with the Rural Home Missionary Association based in our hometown of Morton. When I ran my decision by my pastor back home, Mike Boyle, he stated, "It sounds like a good opportunity, Tom." He added, "But I see they require a one-year internship. So here's an idea—why don't you come back here, make application at RHMA and see how God leads." Mike knew of a church in Washington, Illinois, that wanted a pastoral intern for one year to do outreach Bible studies, work with youth, and do some occasional preaching. Perfect!

Cindi and I felt like we had found the Golden Goose. Interning for the princely sum of $20,000 a year, I was teaching Bible studies, leading youth groups, and having the time of my life. I was working with a veteran pastor, Jim Gross, and he and I became good friends. As the one-year timeframe was coming to an end, the church decided they needed an assistant pastor and they offered me the role.

We loved the people and the role, so Cindi and I gladly agreed to accept the church's offer and gave them a five-year commitment.

Meanwhile, in another part of the greater Peoria area, another church was going through transition. Liberty Bible Church in Eureka had just lost their Senior Pastor. In what felt like an out-of-the-blue offer, I was contacted to see if I would be interested in being a candidate for the position.

"No," I replied, "I just committed to five years at Grace Bible Church in Washington." But Pastor Gross encouraged me to candidate for the experience. He didn't believe that they would offer me the role since I was so inexperienced.

So I did candidate. The following week we were scheduled to go to Washington, D.C., for a vacation with my sister and brother-in-law. I would need a vacation after the Sunday that preceded it. That day I taught a Sunday School class, preached Sunday morning, met with folks all afternoon, preached Sunday evening, had a two hour question-and-answer session, and then jumped in the van, and drove to D.C.—arriving at 2 PM the following afternoon.

The following Saturday, I received a phone call at Bill and Linda's. "Tom, I thought you'd want to know we're voting on you tomorrow night." On that warm summer Sunday night in July of 1988, I was voted in as the Pastor of Liberty Bible Church of Eureka. Now all I had to do was come back and explain everything to the folks at Grace.

They were kind and understanding, so on August 1st I was installed as the new pastor, and I've been there ever since. At the time, the church was meeting in a shopping center. We are now in our fourth building program. God knew what He was doing.

And by the way, God also knew what He was doing when He led us away from Dallas Bible College and toward Calvary. It turns out that Dallas Bible College moved to Tyler, Texas, in the summer of 1985. A year later, the school closed down.

And where did all their students end up going, once the school closed its doors?

They went to Calvary Bible College in Kansas City.

CHAPTER SIX:

THE FUN AND FRENZY OF FIVE KIDS

When Cindi and I got married, we weren't sure that we could have kids. There were some medical issues, so we weren't even using any birth control. After we were married about a year, I can recall the two of us being with our friends Doug and Jan Sherman, from the Navigators. Cindi wasn't feeling real well and as she described her symptoms to Jan, the cause of the ill feelings were summed up in a few words by Jan— "I think you're pregnant!"

"I don't think so," Cindi replied sincerely.

But we made our way over to the Base hospital the next day and they administered the pregnancy test on her and she passed. We were going to be parents!

When we called Cindi's parents, we said to them,
"We're going to have an addition to the family!"

Her mom responded with genuine excitement in her voice,
"Oh, you're getting a puppy!"

Nine months later, August 15, 1979, while I was still in the Air Force, we had our first child—our daughter Jessica Faith. Cindi's delivery was a quick one. I remember I was watching a Texas Rangers baseball game on TV when she came out of the bedroom saying, "I think I'm having contractions."

Since it didn't seem like a big deal, I responded by saying, "Just let me know if it's getting worse and we'll head to the hospital."

When the contractions started arriving every five minutes, we decided it was time to call the hospital. Since we lived about ten minutes from the hospital, they didn't seem to be all that concerned. "When the contractions start coming every two or three minutes, get in here."

An hour later we hit the every-two-minute mark, but remarkably, they were not painful to her. We arrived at the hospital around 10:30 PM that evening. Jessica arrived at 12:50 AM on August 15th, which—by the way—was the due date given us by the doctor. She was our firstborn, and what a blessing she has been! Strong-willed with deep convictions, she is more like her dad than her mom. She became a second mother to her younger siblings and still is today. Trustworthy and faithful, we could always count on Jess. She is the smallest of our kids in size, but is big on leadership. I'm thankful that she met her "Tennessee gentleman," Robert Reeves. An Eagle Scout with a quiet demeanor, he is just what Jess needs; and they have two cute boys, Judson and Wesley.

Twenty-one months later, in May of 1981, we had a baby boy that we named Benjamin Thomas. By then we had completed our time in the Air Force and we were back living in Morton where I was working at the family business. That meant that we were no longer ten minutes from a hospital. It was about 30 minutes, but the doctor told us the second baby may come quicker than the first, which made us a little nervous. I pictured myself delivering our second baby in the back seat of our Cutlass!

The due date for Ben was the first week of June, but ten days before that, Cindi started feeling the contractions. So we made the drive to the hospital at 1 AM just to be on the safe side. The contractions were severe enough that the doctors went ahead and broke Cindi's water, and little baby Ben came along around mid-afternoon on Tuesday, May 26th.

The date of Ben's birthday is significant to me for a couple of reasons. First, it's my half-birthday. I was born on November 26th. It's just one more way I feel connected with one of my kids.

Secondly, and more importantly, as Ben grew up playing baseball, the age cutoff was always May 31st to determine which age he would play with. This means that Ben was always forced to play with the older and bigger boys, which made it harder, thus toughening him up. By the time Ben got to his freshman year of high school, he was playing with seniors he had grown up with, so it was not intimidating to him.

If he had been born on his due date, it would have been after the May 31st cutoff, and it would have been an entirely different experience.

Another interesting tidbit about the day of Ben's birth is that it was on a Tuesday, which meant it was the day of the week when I had a fast-pitch softball game for a league in which I was playing. Now remember, this is back in the days before the father essentially moved into the hospital with the expectant mother. Granted I was up all night with Cindi before Ben was born that afternoon, but once the baby arrived, there wasn't much for me to do.

So I left the hospital after dinner and got back to Morton in plenty of time for our 9 PM start. What makes this story so perfect is that I had the best softball game of my career that night.

- I hit two home runs, one of them being a grand slam!

- I hit a triple with the bases loaded.

- I had eight RBIs in that single game.

All of this occurred while being physically exhausted from having been up all night. But I had a son!

Ben married Julianna Gilmore, the perfect complement to him. I'm thankful for them both, and for how they handle their hectic lifestyles with such grace and humility. They have three beautiful children, Zion, Kruse, and Blaise.

In 1983, we welcomed our second daughter, Serena Joy, on May 4th. She was the only one of our five for which we knew the gender of our baby in advance. She was a blessing! It started with her unique name. With an almost 4-year-old and almost 2-year-old at home, we weren't sure how child number three would be handled. One night, while searching a name book, we came upon the name Serena. It meant 'tranquility' and we thought we could use some of that, so we named her Serena.

The way I describe Serena is that she was the best! I don't ever remember spanking her. I'm sure I must have, but I can't think of one specific incident that would have required it. She is a great daughter and now mom to her own family. She is a lovely person and I love to be around her. As a matter of fact, she may be the nicest person I know!

Equally nice is her quiet husband, Michael Grimm. He is a great husband, dad and all-around leader in his home and in our church. I could not have picked someone more suited for Serena. Michael and Serena live near us—along with their three children, Lucy, Dylan, and Rex—and we love seeing them often!

The day we brought Serena home from the hospital had some drama linked to it. With Cindi in the hospital for a couple of days, that meant that I was in charge of a 4-year-old and a 2-year-old, which was quite a demanding exercise. As I was getting Jess and Ben ready to go to the hospital to pick up their mom and new baby sister, I noticed 2 year-old Ben sitting on the floor of his bedroom eating something mysterious. As I pulled it away from him I discovered it was one of those moisture packets you find in a shoebox. It did not escape my attention as I yanked it from him, that the packet was printed with large words on front and back, DO NOT EAT.

Immediately I called Poison Control. "I just found my 2-year-old son eating a moisture packet from a shoe box. What should I do?"

The voice on the other line didn't seem all that much in a hurry, which really began to bother me. I don't know the actual time involved, but it felt like an hour later he finally found the procedure in one of his handbooks. "It's okay," he announced. "It won't hurt him."

"Why would it be stamped with DO NOT EAT on it?" I fired back in confusion. I'll never forget his answer.

"Because it's not food."

Three kids in six years—wow!

By now we were in Kansas City while I was attending Calvary Bible College. This is difficult to admit, but we didn't really want any more children, at least not at that time. So, when Cindi found out she was pregnant with number four, we were actually angry and bitter toward God. How foolish of us!

The Lord had to teach us a lesson. A painful lesson. We ended up losing that baby during the pregnancy. We learned immediately that we would never ever be ungrateful to God for what He brings into our lives. We had to confess our selfishness and lack of faith and ask Him for His forgiveness. Please understand, I want to make sure that doesn't sound as if everyone that has something like that happen is being disciplined. It's just how we felt at the time. Like we had bad attitudes. This is such an important point and I don't want to be misunderstood, so let me repeat myself—for others that have suffered the loss of a child or pregnancy, it doesn't necessarily mean that God is teaching you a lesson. It's just the way we felt after having been ungrateful. But God's grace prevailed and...

Two years later, in 1988, we welcomed Peter James Zobrist to our family. He came along while I was doing my internship at Grace Bible in Washington. Pete was another indication that having children is not always as easy as the first three of our kids were. Early on in the pregnancy, Cindi spent a week in the hospital from dehydration and morning sickness. Then at seven months, through an ultrasound at a routine appointment, it was discovered that unborn baby Pete had hydronephrosis, or water on the kidney. After a couple of amniocenteses to check for lung maturity, it was decided that he should be delivered early. Fortunately, the problem was easily remedied and Pete has never had kidney problems.

To look at Pete, you would never know there were issues at birth. At 6 feet, 5 inches tall, he is the biggest of our kids and probably has the biggest heart. Pete is a servant and can be counted on when I need help. Strong and willing, he helps me at home when I have dirty jobs to do. He is also a good communicator, frequently checking in throughout the week by phone. At this writing, he is the only one of our kids not married, but that is about to change. The Lord has brought a wonderful girl into his life, Anna Lofquist. Anna is a great complement to Pete in every way. They make a great pair and I look forward to how God will use them.

Six years into my pastorate at Liberty Bible Church, our final child, Noah Andrew, was born in 1994. Noah is a special person, uniquely put together by the Lord. He is missing two fingers on his right hand. That's the way he was born. He's never known any differently and he gets along just fine. I remember when we brought him home from the hospital, on the following Sunday I carried him in my arms up to the pulpit and introduced him to our congregation. I showed them his hand and said, "This is how God made him. Come and look at it and then treat him as you would anyone else." That was it. That's all I had to say.

To this day, Noah doesn't hide his hand, but neither does he flaunt it. I do recall a time or two when he spun a yarn with some of his friends by saying, "An alligator bit off my fingers." But he's a prince of a young man. As I write these words, he is finishing up college at Calvary University and interning as a Youth Pastor and Biblical Counselor at a church in Kansas City. He and his lovely wife Courtney Fleck will be great in whichever ministry God intends for them. They both have a heart for serving God and His people. Right now, Courtney is a nurse; but I know her dream job is to be a church secretary. Sweet Courtney, Noah may be able to arrange that for you someday!

Our frenzied five have expanded to a talented ten! We are blessed with our five in-law children. They all love Jesus, are talented, love our kids, and more than anything, they make our kids better people. They have already given us eight wonderful grandchildren and we hope for even more! We could not be more thankful to the Lord for how He has orchestrated their lives, and we give God all the glory for any good in any of us! Look what God can do!

CHAPTER SEVEN:

LOOK WHAT GOD CAN DO IN SPITE OF ME

One of the main reasons for writing this book is to set the record straight. I get a lot of credit for the success that my son Ben is currently enjoying, and the truth of the matter is that much of what Ben has achieved has been in spite of me as opposed to because of me. Every day, I thank God that He has chosen to use my son in the way that He has. I can see choices that Ben made that were the exact opposite of advice I had given him, yet it turned out to be the right decision. And I can also look back and see how hard I was on him at certain times in his life, for which I needed his forgiveness and God's. I'm so thankful that God's grace can overcome our failures.

One particular example took place when Ben was in the seventh grade. He excelled in all sports, but I recall his prowess in running track. As a seventh grader, he already held the school record for the mile—5:01! Because of this, he was headed to the State track meet, where he would compete in no less than four events; the mile, the 800 meters, the 4 by 200 meters relay, and the high jump. (People were amazed at the specific collection of four events—most milers weren't high jumpers and vice-versa!)

The first day of the State meet was on a Friday, and Ben would be competing in the preliminary rounds for the mile and the high jump. I felt that Ben could medal in the mile. It was more than a feeling. He was ranked third in the state. As I studied the entries, I observed that Ben was placed in the fastest heat. It was all coming together.

"You can do this," I pressed him before his heat. "You can win this race. Go out hard. Take it. You can do it!"

As I think back on those pieces of advice from that day, I feel terrible. Clearly I pushed him too hard. I put a tremendous amount of pressure on a young boy. I wish I would have encouraged him by saying something like, "Now go on out there and run your best, but have some fun!"

1992 E.Y.R.A. Traveling Team

But I didn't.

The runners took their marks and the starting pistol was fired. Ben came out strong, just as I had counseled him to do. The problem was soon apparent—he ran too hard in the beginning and it wasn't too long before he started to fade.

He gave it his best shot, but he was out of gas because of my advice to go out hard. I watched in shock as he came to the final 100 meters of the race and collapsed.

Seeing him sprawled out on the track, at least I responded in the way any good father would have—I jumped the fence to help him up.

But of course, once I did that, he was immediately disqualified because I touched him. I was just glad he was okay.

By the way, the next day he medaled in the 800 meters and the 4 by 200 meters relay.

But I've never forgotten that DQ.

Recently someone asked me if I coached Ben a lot while he was growing up. I responded with, "Yes, I did offer him a lot of coaching. It feels like I was always telling him how he could do it better."

But the more I thought about that question, I found a big smile forming on my face. Why? Because in reality, it was Ben's younger sister, Serena, and brothers, Pete and Noah, who received the lion's share of my coaching of Ben! I can remember car ride after car ride where it was just Serena, Cindi, the younger boys, and me in the vehicle and I waxed eloquent for hours after Ben's games on how he could have improved his overall play. They just sat there, quietly listening, patiently putting up with advice that had nothing to do with them. They let old Dad vent.

When I reflect on my parenting, I have come to the conclusion that I am not an encourager by nature. I am more of an exhorter. And when that exhortation is done truthfully and lovingly, it is a good thing. Compassionate exhorting makes us better. But when it's not administered properly, it can be as deadly as poison. Exhorting can be a blessing or a curse.

But you'll be happy to know I am always trying to improve in my own life. I've tried to be more loving and compassionate, even when it comes to my 'coaching.' I can still remember a conversation I had with Ben, years later, when he was playing college ball at Olivet Nazarene University. We were sitting in a booth at a Steak 'n Shake fast food restaurant. Ben's exact words to me were, "Dad, why don't you yell at me after games anymore?"

It was never Ben's—nor our—dream that Ben play pro baseball; and even if it was, it would not have been for the Cubs, especially being MVP in the World Series. That would have been more of a nightmare! (I was an obnoxious Cardinal fan and taught Ben to be the same.) But when players, coaches and parents learn to do sports God's way, our hearts become moldable so that God can make us what He wants us to be rather than what we think we should be. That was a hard process for me to learn.

During Ben's senior year, Ben's baseball coach Bob Gold told me that he thought Ben could play college baseball. Unfortunately, no schools had approached us with serious offers and we felt better with Ben going to Calvary Bible College, (now Calvary University), where I had gone to school, and pursuing some sort of ministry since he had some gifts in that area. We, as his parents, felt like we had a good plan for his life, he just needed to trust us and he would be blessed. How horrible does that sound? But as I observe families, I sometimes see similar situations.

It is well documented that Ben spent $50 of his birthday money to go to a tryout camp in June after he graduated. I was not going to spend the money because he was supposed to be leaving for a church youth convention that day, and because I felt nothing lasting would come out of it. We had a plan; He was committed to Calvary Bible College, and if he wanted to play with his friends, there were easier ways. But I relented and let him go. Long story short, out of that tryout came several calls from coaches and one full scholarship offer for Ben to pitch for Olivet Nazarene University and Coach Elliot Johnson. We were out of town, so Coach Gold accompanied Ben to visit. Bob told me he felt it was something we should consider. Coach Johnson was a committed Christian and he really wanted Ben, Bob said. So the next week, we reluctantly went to visit with Ben. We sat in Coach Johnson's office and he told us Ben would pitch immediately and "maybe" get a chance to play other positions, but he made no promises. He also said that he emphasized discipleship. At that moment, a young couple just "coincidentally" happened by. I believe in God's sovereignty, since there are no coincidences with God. Coach introduced us to Dan and Liz Heefner. Dan was to be a mature senior on the Olivet team and Coach said he would like Dan to disciple Ben. Dan and Liz were newlyweds and eventually would play a key role in Ben meeting Julianna, his wife, since Liz was Julianna's older sister. (Dan is now Dallas Baptist University's head coach and one of the top college coaches in the nation.) Despite all this, we were skeptical, and it was now July and there was not a lot of time to think or to pray.

So we went to Cracker Barrel in Kankakee and discussed what was happening. Cindi was very emotional, since this was sending shockwaves through the plans we had for our son. I was torn between my love for God, my wife, Ben, and baseball as to what I should do.

I asked Ben if he had prayed about it and what he thought. He was 19 years old and was getting ready to go away to school. He was going to make his own decisions and I could not be there for him every minute. (That was before texting.) It was time for him to practice what he had learned about prayer and following God; about submission to His will not his own. He answered, "I don't believe I'm done playing baseball yet, but if you think it's the right thing for me to go to Calvary, I will go to Calvary." I knew at that moment that if he could be submissive to me, he was ready to be submissive to God. And so, he started at Olivet just a few weeks later.

Three years passed, and another transition took place where God took Ben to another level. He was playing baseball in the Northwoods League in Wausau, Wisconsin, and his roommate was a young man from Dallas Baptist, a program that was transitioning to Division 1 the next year. Jeff, by another divine coincidence, was Julianna's brother. By the way, Ben and Julianna were not dating yet. Interestingly enough, Jeff told Ben they could use a shortstop. When the DBU coach was visiting Jeff that summer, Ben called and asked if I would come meet him. I drove up that day and met with Coach Mike Bard and the Woodchucks coach, Steve Foster, who is now the Rockies pitching coach. (Steve thought Ben should have been drafted and couldn't understand why it had not happened yet. He thought it was because God needed to get him a wife first, since they are hard to find after one starts in pro ball! That's a whole other story.)

Both coaches are strong believers. While we were meeting in the bowels of this old field, Ben approached us and asked if we had his life planned for him yet. I again wanted to control the situation. I discouraged the transfer. Olivet had been good to him. He had much success there. He was an All-American, two trips to the NAIA World Series; what more could he want? He said, "Dad, I have one year left to play baseball. I want to see what I can do against the best players possible." He wanted to play a D-1 schedule. So, with a little encouragement from Ned Yost, whose son would be one of Ben's roommates, we let Ben transfer to DBU for his senior year. I say "we" sarcastically, since we were controlling nothing. One year later he was drafted in the 6th round by the Houston Astros.

Looking back, I can see that God was working the whole time transitioning Ben and us gently from the safety of our home and little church and little community to being able to survive and thrive in the world of professional baseball. Ben had learned through that transition that God had to be number one and that baseball was an avenue to serving Him, not an end in itself. The night before he left for Albany, New York, and his rookie-league assignment with the Tri-City Valley Cats, as he lay in bed, I sat on the edge and we prayed together. He told me not to worry; that he was going to play in the big leagues and he was going to be a missionary to the people he had contact with there. "I'll be like any other missionary, but I won't need financial support. But I do need prayer." God had prepared us to let him go where we never would have four years before. Look what God has done in spite of ourselves!

From 2004 through 2006, Ben played minor league ball in the Astros organization. He played low-A ball, A ball, high-A ball, and AA ball before he was traded to the Tampa Bay Rays in 2006. The Rays sent him to their AAA team, the Durham Bulls (the team made famous by the Kevin Costner movie Bull Durham).

Midway through that season, July 31 to be precise, my phone rang and I answered to hear a very excited son on the other end of the line. "Hey Dad, we're going up to the Big Leagues!"

Ben would move back and forth from AAA and the majors for three seasons; 2006, when he was up about one-third of the season; 2007, again, up about one-third of the season; and then 2008, when he was up for two-thirds of the season. From 2009 on, he's never been back down, unless he was doing a stint for the rehab of an injury.

And it was 2006, when he moved over to the Tampa Bay Rays organization, that Ben began a relationship that is maintained to this day. For nine of the ten years Ben has been in the majors, he has been playing for a fascinating individual named Joe Maddon, of whom I will have more to say as we continue.

The exception to those years with Joe was 2015. A crazy year that would ultimately end in a World Series victory. Ben's first, but not his last.

CHAPTER EIGHT:

WEARING LOTS OF HATS

The year 2015 proved to be a year unlike any other.

I vividly recall a conversation I had with Ben over Christmas the year before, where he posed a hypothetical question to me that I didn't take very seriously. "Dad, what if I signed with the Cubs? With Joe (Maddon) there now as their manager, they might try to sign me when I am a free agent next year."

The backstory is that we knew a trade was likely in the works. Ben would be a free agent after 2015 and Tampa Bay was ready to deal Ben at some point before the end of the year and no one knew exactly where that meant he might end up.

Well, the trade occurred and it wasn't to the Cubs. Less than a month later, in January of 2015 Ben called with the announcement. "Hey Dad, we got traded to Oakland."

"Wow!" was the only response I could think of to give back to him.

"Yeah," he continued with a laugh, "It looks like God has something for us in Oakland."

As I hung up the phone, Cindi made her opinion clear to me. "Oakland? That's a longer flight than flying to Tampa? What's going on?"

In our minds, there was nothing good about Oakland. Apologies to anyone who lives in that area, but that's just the way we felt at the time. It was so far from home!

Our bad vibes were only increased by the rough start Ben experienced as a member of that team. In April they were on the road, playing the Royals in Kansas City, when Ben went down with a knee injury—a meniscus tear. Minor surgery took care of the problem, along with the appropriate amount of time to heal, recover, and rehabilitate.

I called to check in on him once he was released from the hospital. He was far from upbeat. "Hey Son, how's it going?"

Ben was laying on an air mattress, alone in their apartment, numb from the knee down. Julianna, the kids and their furniture had not yet arrived. Alcatraz was right outside the window, but Ben right now was in his own little prison. Alone, unable to walk, and unsure of his immediate future.

As parents, we wanted to help, we wanted to be there; but all we could do was pray. But that's what he needed right at that moment.

Ben was having a rough start.

Cindi and I decided to fly out to see him for his birthday in May, and I was to discover that you just couldn't keep a good man down. By mid-May Ben was back in the Oakland lineup and he was playing well.

That was the first part of the 2015 season. As the trade deadline of July 31st loomed closer, it looked like Ben may be traded once again. And we were correct.

The last week of July, 2015, I received a text from Ben that was all of two characters in length. He simply texted "KC."

"Are you kidding me?" I texted back immediately.

Another two character reply: "No."

And with that announcement, Ben became a member of the Royals.

Not only did the trade get Ben out of Oakland and to a geographic area much closer to us, something even better was happening: The day Ben joined the Royals, they were in first place with a ten-game lead over their closest competitor! Kansas City had a strong team—they were in the World Series the year before, losing in seven games to the San Francisco Giants. On top of that, Ben had a history with Ned Yost, the Royals manager. You know from a previous chapter the relationship that he had with Ned, and he roomed with Ned Jr. at Dallas Baptist.

It was a happy time all around.

Ben started out with a bang with the Royals. On his first road trip he hit a couple of home runs!

The fans loved Ben and Ben loved the fans. "Some of my earliest memories were being taken to the Royals games at the 'K' (short for Kauffman Field)," he would recall for the local fans and media. It was the truth and the community just ate it up.

The Royals made the playoffs, where they beat the Toronto Blue Jays in six games. With that victory, they won their way to the World Series, where they ended up defeating the New York Mets in five games.

It's at this point that I would love to give you a heartwarming recollection of the Victory Parade in Kansas City. The truth, however, is that the parade was a nightmare for Cindi and me. We got trapped in the middle of a huge crowd and so the reality is that we didn't see one second of the parade. I can tell you a great deal about the people surrounding me, but that is of no consequence to our story.

It was after the parade that day that Ben raised a fascinating question to me. "How do you top this?" he asked, referring of course, to the World Series win. "Win one with the Cardinals?" he added with a smile, knowing my hardcore devotion to the St. Louis team.

I think my answer surprised him. "No, it's not winning one with the Cards," I answered. "It would be winning one with the Cubs!"

"Really?"

"Sure. Think about it," I explained. "The Cardinals have won the championship several different times, so it's not that big of a deal. But if you won the World Series with the Cubs," I paused for maximum effect, "That would be legendary.

"But what's most important is doing what God wants you to do. That's what is going to bring joy and satisfaction to your life."

And that's what I believe, and I know that's what Ben believes. So isn't it ironic that people are always going to remember who was the Most Valuable Player for the Chicago Cubs the year they finally won the World Series?

Who says God doesn't have a sense of humor?

It was early December of 2015. I remember it well, because Noah was getting married on Saturday the 5th. Ben and Julianna were with us in Eureka, the week before and I remember him asking me how long it would take them to get to the Peoria Airport. I told him to plan on an hour and he nodded saying, "That'll work."

"What time is your flight?" I asked.

"It's taking off in a little over an hour," he replied.

I furrowed my brow and said, "Well you'll need more time to get through security and all the other stuff, don't you think?"

"Not a problem, Dad," he answered. "We're actually flying on a private jet, so we won't need to do all that stuff."

"A private jet?" I repeated.

"Yeah, it belongs to the president of the New York Mets. They want to fly us out to New York to take a look around," was his explanation. "We're going to see the field, some neighborhoods in Connecticut. I think they're wanting to wine and dine us."

"Don't forget Noah's wedding," was all I could think of to say.

"We'll be back tonight by 10 PM," he replied.

As they were leaving Ben took me aside and whispered, "Dad, if you want me to play for the Cubs, you better pray." And with that they were gone.

They returned Thursday night, and on Saturday we enjoyed having the whole family together for the wedding of Noah and his bride, Courtney.

On Sunday, Ben and Julianna were gone once again. This time it was to the West Coast. He was now being courted by the San Francisco Giants. They really wanted him, and so they rolled out the red carpet treatment. Somewhere in that whole mix was strong interest from the Washington Nationals, too.

They flew back Monday evening and the plan was for them to land in St. Louis. The full plan was that we would drive down to a tiny town in southern Illinois named Lebanon, and there we would pass off the kids back to Ben and Jules, who would go from there to their home in Nashville. It may sound confusing, but it knocked off some miles for their family to have to drive.

So imagine my surprise when my cell phone rang that Monday night and I heard Ben on the other end. "Dad, we're at St. Louis Airport and we can't get our car to start. Can you come down and help us out?"

I was dumbfounded. "Have you checked the battery?" I asked.

"Yeah," he answered.

"How about the starter? Or the alternator?"

"Dad, can you just come to the airport?" was all that Ben was saying.

"Isn't there a mechanic at the parking lot that can help?" I asked in desperation."

"Dad, please come," Ben pleaded.

So that's how we ended up driving to St. Louis. All the way down there, Cindi and the grandkids got an earful from me about how lame the maintenance department must be at that parking garage. And how could I have a son who makes so much money, but he doesn't have a decent car?

When we ultimately arrived at the parking lot, I stopped as we entered and told the gatekeeper that we were in need of some assistance with a car that wouldn't start.

"Just let me know the location of the vehicle and we'll get someone out there right away," the attendant volunteered.

"So why couldn't Ben have done the same thing?" I muttered to myself as we pulled into the lot. Eventually we found their vehicle and I was surprised to see that the engine must have been running since there was exhaust belching out of the exhaust pipe below. Now I was really confused.

Ben got out of the car with Jules right behind him.

"What's the deal?" I demanded, having utterly run out of Christian love and patience.

"I kinda had to tell a little lie," Ben began sheepishly.

"Go on," I pressed.

"Well, we have decided where we want to play next year and we wanted to tell you both in person," was his explanation. By now both Cindi and I perked up our ears. "We really liked it in San Francisco," he said as he watched our shoulders slump.

"It's too far away," I heard Cindi whisper to no one in particular.

Once they could see they had our undivided attention, they made the big announcement. "We did like San Francisco, BUT we have decided to sign with the Cubs for $56 million dollars!"

We immediately broke into the Walk-off Dance.

"I can't believe you're excited that I'm a Cub," Ben admitted.

"I'm a Cub fan now!" I beamed with pride.

So this announcement, though still a secret, caused us to totally rework our travel plan. Ben still had to pass a physical and the exam was to be conducted right away up in Chicago. To help Julianna with the kids, Cindi volunteered to drive down to Nashville with her, even though all she had with her were the clothes on her back. We buckled in the kids, sent the ladies off and then got Ben to Chicago.

These changes left me driving back to Eureka alone with nothing to do but listen to the MLB network on my radio. "Where's Ben Zobrist going?" was a topic for discussion that came up on the network while I was driving.

"He's going to the Mets," one listener offered.

"Nope, it's the Nationals."

"You watch, the Giants are going to sign him!"

I found myself wanting to shout out loud, "He's going to the Cubs, but nobody knows it yet!" Ben wanted to return playing for Joe Maddon. And he wanted the challenge of beating the curse.

The next day I was back at home while Cindi was returning from Nashville and Ben was having his physical exam. I checked my calendar and I was scheduled to attend a school concert that evening for my granddaughter Lucy, so off I went. It was in the middle of the concert that the call from Ben arrived. I got up and went out into the hallway.

Dad, I passed everything, so the Cubs will probably make the announcement tonight.

No sooner had I returned to my seat when phones started being alerted around me with an alert from MLB: Zobrist signs with Cubs.

What was especially entertaining was to observe how many folks in the audience received the same alert at the same time. People were turning around, looking at me with big smiles on their faces—if they were Cubs fans. The Cardinal fans in the crowd turned around too, with scowls as big as the smiles on the Cubs fans.

When the concert ended, I was mobbed with folks wanting to hear what I thought about the big news. There were even people who wanted their picture taken with me. A Peoria newspaper reporter called to do an interview with me. It felt like overnight I went from this quiet life to a person everyone wanted to know everything about.

To this day, I refer to it as the Cub effect. It's a real deal.

CHAPTER NINE:

WORLD SERIES GAME SEVEN: THE MVP

Two months later, in February of 2016, Ben was off to Mesa, Arizona, for Cubs spring training. He was signed to play second base, but we knew that Joe Maddon would use Ben as he needed him, which turned out to be correct.

By now it's cliché to call the 2016 Cubs season 'miraculous' or 'magical,' but there's almost no other way to describe it. Take the All-Star Game as an example. The entire Cubs infield was chosen for the National League team—amazing! And that included Ben playing at second base. The game was held in San Diego, and you can be sure Cindi and I were in attendance. Beyond the thrill of having a son in the All-Star Game, San Diego itself is a gorgeous spot. "We have to come back here for a vacation," I suggested to Cindi, underscoring how much I was really enjoying it.

For Cindi and me, the entire season was an exciting time. Everyone we knew wanted to talk about the Cubs. And since they were in first place from the first day of the season, people were constantly chattering about the amazing accomplishment and how we were in the midst of a great sports feat.

As the season progressed, Ben started playing in some different positions. On occasion he would be out in right field, so that Joe could get Javier Báez in at second base. During the playoffs, Ben was moved to left field and it was in left field that he ended up staying.

In the Division Series, we won over the Giants three games to one. Then in the League Championship Series, we came back from a 2-1 deficit to beat the Dodgers four games to two.

Cindi and I attended all the home games in the Cubs playoff schedule, but none of the away games. That would change when the Cubs made it to the World Series. We saw all seven games—three at Wrigley and four at Progressive Field in Cleveland—up close and personal.

The Indians beat us on their home turf to take a 1-0 lead; but we came back the next night and beat them, creating a 1-1 tie. Game Three was in our beloved Wrigley Field, but we lost it 1-0. To make it worse, we lost the next night in a 7-2 loss, which put us at an unenviable 3-1 deficit. Game Five at Wrigley went our way and we won it 3-2. So it was back to Cleveland with the task of winning them both on the road. We were ready for Game Six—a 9-3 whipping of the Indians.

It all came down to Game 7.

There's a lot that can be said about the entire series. But of course, my strongest memories come from that historic Game Seven. The Cubs management was extremely supportive of the families of the players, and one of the ways they showed it was by providing family members with bus transportation to and from all the away games over in Cleveland.

Even the weather in Cleveland on that Wednesday evening, November 2nd, should have given us a clue that this was going to be an unusual night. We had all come prepared with our winter clothes for the predictably chilly temperatures to be expected at that time of year. To our amazement, the evening was nice and warm, a bit muggy, but definitely short-sleeved weather. I ended up going to the game in jeans and a Zobrist jersey, without even carrying a coat.

Even though we were on the road, I felt really good about our chances of winning the championship game. I felt like we had the upper hand, especially after the stomping we put on them during Game Six. I also was aware of a key statistic that would work in our favor—I had heard a stat that if the Cubs faced a pitcher a third time in 2016, the pitcher's earned run average skyrocketed to over 7. In other words, by the third time, the Cubs figured out what the pitcher had and learned how to hit him. And we were looking at Indian pitcher Corey Kluber for the third time in a week!

Another hint that we were in for something special was the fact that our first batter, center fielder Dexter Fowler, hit the fourth pitch straight over the right-center field fence! It was the first time anyone had led off a seventh game of a World Series with a home run.

The Indians tied it up in the third but we came right back with a two run fourth inning. We were up 3-1 and then in the fifth we scored another two runs so that we had a 5-1 lead, which seemed comfortable. But the key word I guess was 'seemed.'

Cubs pitcher Kyle Hendricks was still looking good to most of us in the bottom of the fifth inning, when to the surprise of most fans, Joe Maddon pulled him in favor of Jon Lester. It didn't go the Cubs' way at that point with Cleveland scoring two more runs to make it 5-3. We scored another run in the sixth to make it 6-3.

In the eighth inning, Joe brought in Aroldis Chapman to relieve Lester. Once again, it didn't go our way. The Indians scored one run, and then Rajai Davis hit a two-run homer off of Chapman to tie it up in the eighth.

I remember looking at Cindi and uttering, "Oh my word...."

That was an important moment for me. I can recall vividly thinking to myself, "I have not known what it has meant to be a 'suffering Cubs fan.' I had grown up a Cardinals fan, so I didn't have to suffer. They'd win a pennant every few years, so it was no big deal." But when Davis hit that home run, I remember thinking to myself, "Now I know. Now I, too, am a suffering Cubs fan."

In the ninth inning, Chapman escaped unscathed and it looked like we were going into extra innings. But it also looked like it was going to rain. And it did just that—it came down in full force. The umpires wisely called a rain delay as the players hustled back through the dugouts to the clubhouse. There is a room underneath the stands in every stadium reserved for the player's families, so that is where Cindi and I headed. The rain delay was short, only seventeen minutes. It was during that seventeen minutes that the Cubs had an unofficial players-only team meeting, their first of the year. Jason Heyward gave a pep talk to the team that was just the right motivation for the Cubs to pull it all together.

I was watching the field on a TV in the stadium's family room, when I noticed they were starting to remove the tarps. We headed back up to our seats as the game was beginning to resume.

Kyle Schwarber hit a single and Joe put in Albert Almora, Jr. as a pinch runner. Kris Bryant flied out deep to center field, allowing Almora to tag and go to second. I knew what that meant. The Indians chose to walk Rizzo intentionally, and in doing so that meant they preferred to take their chances pitching to Ben. Trying to be objective, I must say that was a smart baseball move. Almora had already made it to second, so putting Rizzo on would set up a force out.

These are the moments a player lives for! The Cubs fans were going crazy and it's important to note that the stadium was split about half and half with Cubs fans and Indians fans. We were loud and proud!

I was trying to maintain my composure.

Can you even imagine the pressure that was on Ben? Later he would tell the press: "I was just as nervous as anyone else would be going up there. They intentionally walked (Rizzo) to get to me, so there's a part of you that your pride is a little hurt that they'd rather face you than that guy. Kind of makes you want to really, really do it at that point...I had to block out all the emotion. If you try to be the hero in that situation, it never works out."

The first pitch was high: ball 1. The second pitch was a perfect strike: 1-1. The third pitch was another strike, and now Ben was down 1-2. The fourth pitch was up and away, and Ben took an emergency hack so it remained 1-2.

And then there was the fifth pitch. Ben connected for a solid double down the left field line, scoring Almora.

All along I had been mumbling a sincere prayer, "May God be glorified," along with, "I pray he (Ben) will glorify You."

My response to his hit? I'm a little embarrassed to admit it, but just so you don't think I'm some super-spiritual saint, beyond my muttered prayer I also cried aloud, "Who are we gonna bring in to pitch the bottom of the 10th?"

Looking back, I think that's kind of sad. Here are all the Cubs fans, screaming and hugging during this once-in-a-lifetime moment, and all I could think about was the rest of the game!

But Ben came through! Later he tried to describe his feelings to the press:

> "I was really uncomfortable. He got me down. I was just flailing at balls, just taking an emergency hack. And then the last one was just over the plate and up enough that I could get enough of the barrel to it.
>
> When I hit it, I think I lost consciousness. I didn't remember anything until I was jumping at second base. We felt we knew right then that we were going to win the game. It was just a matter of time to get those last three outs."

Ben's hit was followed by another intentional walk, followed by an RBI single by Miguel Montero. The Cubs scored two runs in the tenth, leaving Ben on third when the side was retired.

Joe brought in Carl Edwards, Jr. to pitch the bottom of the tenth. He got two outs before giving up a run to the Indians. That made it 8-7 with two out. Edwards was replaced by Mike Montgomery. He faced Michael Martinez, forcing him to hit a ground ball right to Kris Bryant at third base, who fielded it with ease.

Just another routine out. Right.

It opened the floodgates like nothing I have ever experienced in my life.

We followed all the other Cub families onto the field in jubilant celebration, and it wasn't long before we connected with Ben. I jumped into his arms and he held me like a baby. We were laughing almost uncontrollably, with Ben occasionally saying, "It's unbelievable!"

Like a doggy following his master, we tagged along behind Ben for the rest of that evening. We watched him being interviewed by television and print media and be named MVP of the 2016 World Series! While waiting, we took our picture with Bill Murray.

The game took place on the night of November 2nd. But due to the rain delay, it ended at around 1 AM on November 3rd. We made our way back to Chicago later that day, because November 4th was the day of the big Cubs Victory Parade.

Everyone was overwhelmed by the parade. Just as the Cubs management made arrangements for us to have bus rides in Cleveland, they insisted that families be included in the Parade. There were an awful lot of Zobrists on that red double decker bus riding down the Magnificent Mile that fantastic Friday.

I was moved by the entire experience. Not only was there a huge turnout numerically, but also to see the faces of people so joyful that tears were streaming down their cheeks was an unforgettable sight. So many Cubs fans were connecting this victory to parents or grandparents that had already passed on. It was like a win for those fans who had gone before, faithfully enduring all those years without a championship.

Cubs fans are truly one of a kind. Their love for their team is like no other. Who else looks forward to sitting around the stadium ten minutes after a win just to sing a corny song entitled "Go Cubs Go!" Wrigley Field is a great place to watch a baseball game, that's for certain. For a guy who grew up a rabid Cardinals fan, I guess I'm having a change of heart.

Go Cubs Go!

CHAPTER TEN:

WATCHING BEN WITH UNCLE NOAH

Every Zobrist I know is now a diehard Chicago Cubs fan.

Well, that might be a bit exaggerated, since for so long many were rabid St. Louis Cardinals fans.

So let me say it this way: Every Zobrist I know is a diehard Ben Zobrist fan. I've got uncles and aunts, nieces and nephews, as well as brothers and sisters and cousins who somehow are able to stop the world around them in order to check in on how the Cubs are doing and what kind of game Ben is having. Some are more casual observers, but others watch with the intensity of the most devoted of fans. They've got their iPad in hand, with the box score or lineup card clearly displayed and instantly updated. It's the coolest thing to watch how Ben has brought the Zobrist family together even closer than they've ever been before. And believe me, we are a tight-knit bunch.

Let me give you an example. At 88 years old, my Uncle Noah is one of Ben's biggest fans.

Uncle Noah is one of my father's younger brothers. My dad died when I was just a kid, so in many respects, Uncle Noah is like a father to me. There were ten kids in my Grandpa's family, six boys and four girls. Born in 1921, my dad was the second-oldest of the boys. My oldest Uncle, Ray, was born blind. Eight years later, Uncle Noah came along in

1929. Uncle Noah grew up and joined the Air Force, serving our country for 22 years in Korea and in Vietnam. Once out of the service, he landed in Mobile, Alabama, where he began working in the hotel industry. He rose up the ladder, ultimately becoming the General Manager of the prestigious Grand Hotel on the Alabama coast, where he served for another 22 years. Uncle Noah could tell you dozens of stories of famous movie stars, athletes, and politicians who enjoyed the blessing of anonymity provided by the hotel, along with its first-class amenities.

Uncle Noah still lives in Alabama with his wife, Dottie. Recently, however, the two of them found their way up to Chicago to attend one of Ben's games in person. They ended up staying over for an extra couple of days, so Uncle Noah and I arranged to watch a Cubs game together in his hotel room. Barry, another friend of mine, was in from out of town so I invited him to join us. The room was more like a suite as the three of us settled into comfortable overstuffed chairs in front of a big screen TV. Uncle Noah was in his normal get-up: a beautiful V-necked sweater over a blue oxford button-down shirt, with blue jeans and comfortable shoes. And his ball cap, proudly proclaiming "Korea and Vietnam Veteran" on the front.

I introduced Barry to Uncle Noah as the Cubs game began. During a lull in the game, Barry said to Uncle Noah, "Tell me a little bit about the Zobrist family." Without realizing it, Barry had struck the motherlode. He was in for an education.

"Tom's dad was named Alpha, and he was known as The Quiet Zobrist," Uncle Noah volunteered as he began reflecting. "The rest of us all had big mouths," he said with a wink and a grin. "Of course, no one knew him as Alpha. We all knew him as Zib. Everyone called him Zib," Uncle Noah repeated for emphasis.

Looking over at me, he continued. "Tom, since your dad was one of the oldest and we were all growing up in the Depression, Pop put Zib to work when Zib was a youngster—like 12 or 13. I can still remember your dad driving a milk truck back and forth from Morton to Pekin. And he was only 12." As we let that thought sink in fully, Uncle Noah added wryly, "Driver's licenses just weren't that important back then."

I picked up on what he was saying. "You remember it well, Uncle Noah, because he would enlist your help, right?"

"That's right, Tom," he agreed. "He would milk the cows, then load the truck, then throw me in the back so that when he got to a delivery, I could jump off and run the order up to the door."

"That's what I thought," I replied.

Suddenly Uncle Noah was no longer talking about the Great Depression, but instead it was the opposing pitcher on TV against the Cubs. "I don't like tall pitchers," Uncle Noah volunteered, completely changing the subject. "Psychologically, they overpower you."

We sat quietly for a moment, then inexplicably, Uncle Noah was back on the milk truck.

"Of course, on days when he was collecting the money, Zib ran the milk up to the door himself," Uncle Noah recalled. "I don't think he really trusted me with any cash."

He paused long enough to watch a pitch or two of the Cubs game, along with a shot of the Cubs dugout. "I don't understand why Joe Maddon wears that beard," Uncle Noah said with a groan and a shake of his head. "He looks like an old man to me."

Barry and I snuck a wink as Uncle Noah returned to Zobrist family stories. "Zib worked his hind end off for the sake of the family and you know what? He never complained. Not once. Our mom saw to it every night at supper that Pop and Zib were the first two served around our table. Every cent Zib made he handed over to Pop and Mom for the family. That's the kind of guy he was."

Uncle Noah stared ahead at the TV, but you could tell his mind had taken him back to his childhood. "Zib dropped out of school before he ever finished the eighth grade. He was really something. Of course he learned it from our dad—he dropped out of school in the sixth grade and he went on to build the most successful construction business in the entire area."

Just like that the subject was changed. "That move always looks like a balk to me," he complained as the opposing pitcher made a move toward the runner on second base.

"If you start toward first, you have to throw it," I explained, "but you can move toward second or third and not be forced to throw it."

"And that's not a balk?"

"Nope."

"Well what do you know?" Uncle Noah exclaimed. "I still learn something new every day," as he looked over at Barry with a twinkle in his eye.

He pulled his hat off to scratch an itch on top of his head. Looking at the word 'Veteran" on his hat, Uncle Noah had a new thought. "Zib was one of the few men who didn't enlist in the army when World War II broke out," he said. "He felt he could be of more help to the family if he stayed home and worked in order to provide for the family. Of course, eventually he was drafted along with my brother Calvin. Zib was sent to Germany and Calvin served in India."

Pausing just long enough to catch his breath, he added. "Thankfully, both of them came back home."

Returning to the game for a moment, he added commentary to the score, which currently had the Cubs down by a run. "I don't understand," he complained, "Whenever we score first, they always let 'em score in the next inning. And it's just happening too many times." He shook his head for emphasis.

"Barry, did you know that Stars and Stripes newspaper told all about Zib's exploits as a softball player in Germany after the war?"

"I did not know that," Barry admitted.

"After the war, he played Kitten Ball (16 inch) and they played without gloves. Well, one day, they hit one deep in the outfield where Zib was playing and he ran as hard as he could but was still not where he needed to be. It ended up coming down behind him, but do you know what? Zib caught that big old Kitten Ball behind his back! None of us could believe it!"

Still thinking about that story, he added, "It's hard to tell a story without putting a little pride into it," he said as his voice trailed off.

"You know Tom, your dad married the prettiest girl in all of Morton. Shirley was beautiful and popular and she was a cheerleader."

This was followed by Uncle Noah observing an opposing batter with hair flowing down his back. "This guy's got a good swing," he commented, "but he really needs a haircut."

Uncle Noah turned to Barry. "Did you know that the Morton School District had the best teachers around?"

Barry shook his head.

"They were great," he continued. "They were all women, no men teachers. And they were all German."

"Why are you going for the fences when all we need is a hit?" he cried at a Cubs batter, interrupting his own stories. "I thought we'd have another run by now."

He turned to Tom. "Can you tell me why it is that sometimes we can run up 12 or 13 runs and then other times we can't buy a hit?"

I just looked at him and shrugged my shoulders.

"I'm surprised they don't have this guy bunting in this situation," I said to no one in particular.

"Some guys just can't bunt," Uncle Noah proclaimed. And then, to show his true colors, he added, "Ben can bunt!"

"Barry, did you know I wrote press releases for the Mobile newspapers? I also wrote features for *Field and Stream, Southern Living* and *Golf Magazine*. I'm not so much a writer as I am a story teller," he confessed.

"That's the very best kind of writing," I chimed in, to Uncle Noah's great pleasure.

After a close pitch, I ventured my own opinion. "That pitch was a strike," I said.

"No it wasn't," Uncle Noah argued.

"It was."

"I disagree. It was inside."

It got quiet for a moment before Uncle Noah spoke once again. "The last time I saw Zib and Tom together was right before I shipped out to Vietnam. What year did your Dad pass away?" he asked.

"1967."

And with that remark, it was quiet once more.

After a few silent moments, Uncle Noah turned to me and said, "Tom, the smartest thing you ever did was put a ball diamond in your backyard."

As if on cue, Ben stepped to the plate and hit a perfect single to shallow right field.

"That's my boy," Uncle Noah mumbled softly. "That's my boy."

Proverbs 20:29 states, "The glory of the young is their strength; the gray hair of experience is the splendor of the old."

I am so grateful for people like Uncle Noah who can speak into my life even at this stage. As long as there is someone older than me, there are lessons that I can be learning.

There is much to be gained by learning from our elders.

Our world today tends to discard our seniors, rather than honor them. In Old Testament times it was different. Consider this Proverb:

The silver-haired head is a crown of glory,
If it is found in the way of righteousness.
—Proverbs 16:31

Spending an afternoon with someone as wise as Uncle Noah is a gift from the Lord. Like all the rest of us, he has his quirks and his opinions, but in many ways that just makes him more lovable. And who knows, us younger folk may be able to teach our elders a little something along the way...

...like additional insight into what constitutes a balk.

CHAPTER ELEVEN:

A VISIT WITH MOM AND LINDA

The summer heat had not yet kicked in the Wednesday morning I went to see my mother. The day before it was a scorcher, and weather reports from nearby Chicago warned of intense thunderstorms heading our way and lasting through the weekend. All that to say it was just another typical July day in our neck of the woods.

Mom lives in a complex for seniors called The Villas of Hollybrook in Morton, not too far from Linda and Bill. I get over to see Mom as often as I can, but it's really my sisters, Linda, Kathy and Emily who spend the most time with her. I mentioned to my sister that I wanted to talk with Mom about some of her memories of the family and put them in my book. Linda responded, "That sounds like a good idea, Tom, but let me go over and make sure she's all prepared for your visit." Linda paused, then added, "A ninety-one-year-old woman needs just a little more time to get ready than the rest of us do."

I pulled up to the Center's parking lot a little before 10 on that muggy midweek morning. I strolled into the main lobby, signed in, and walked down the hall to Mom's place. Knocking on her door, I entered what some would call an apartment, but in reality it is a shrine to the baseball expertise of Ben Zobrist. A poster of Ben playing for the Oakland A's hangs on the inside of the front door. Next to the door is a bulletin board with a pennant of Ben from his Kansas City Royals days hanging adjacent to a Chicago newspaper article entitled "The Curious Case of Ben Zobrist," featuring a color picture of him in his Cubs uniform, taking a cut at a pitch. Directly across from the wall with the bulletin board is the wall with the official Ben Zobrist Chicago Cubs jersey, good old number 18 hung on a coat hanger and strategically positioned so that no one can miss it. Add in a 'W' sign, signifying a Cubs win, a Cubs coffee mug, and a few random newspaper clippings held to the wall by push pins and you're beginning to get the picture. My Mom is a huge Ben Zobrist fan.

To be fair to the rest of her family, I should also point out that on the front of her refrigerator, Mom prominently displays pictures of her kids, grandkids, and great-grandkids. I recently did a quick count and I came up with photos of 50 great-grandchildren lined up neatly in rows of eight or nine on the fridge door.

Even at this stage of her life, Mom is still beautiful. I found myself thinking back to Uncle Noah's comment as I looked at her dressed smartly in a black top with fresh white slacks, "Tom, your Dad married the most beautiful girl in Morton—she was a cheerleader!"

I said a quick hello to Linda, and as the three of us sat down on comfortable chairs in Mom's living room, I began to fire away with my questions. "Dad was four years older than you, right Mom?" I began.

"That's correct," she replied.

"How old were you two when you started dating?" I followed.

"Your dad was twenty and I was sixteen." There was silence for a moment until Mom added, "Back then we didn't think about age differences. It was as simple as my family liked him and my family liked his family."

"Mom, remind Tom about your dating and Dad going off to the war," Linda chimed in helpfully.

"We dated for about a year and then Zib left in September of 1942 to go into the Army. He had a few furloughs that brought him back to visit. I graduated high school in May of 1944 and we were married in July of that same year. Once we were married I went with him to Fort Benning,

Georgia, then he went to Newfoundland until he got his orders to go to Europe in February of 1945. The war was soon over and he came back for good in the spring of '46. He was one of the last U.S. soldiers in Germany. That's where he had his baseball team that he played with for a year. When he came home he went to work for his dad. In December of 1947, we had our first child—Linda." As she said Linda's name, she turned and smiled her way and I could only imagine what that smile truly signified.

"After Linda we had two more daughters, Kathy and Emily, and then our two sons, Tom and Matt."

"What do you remember about my coming into your life?" I asked curiously.

"Well, I remember that your dad really wanted a boy and the girls all loved having a baby brother around."

"And you were six before Matt came along," Linda reminded me.

"Then Zib died," Mom said in a tone that brought quiet in the room for a few extra seconds.

"How did you get through it, Mom?" I asked. "Five young kids and you were suddenly a single mother!"

"I know how she did it," Linda remarked and she looked at Mom as the both of them said in unison, "The Good Lord!"

Mom confessed, "It had to be the Good Lord. Honestly, I didn't think Tom and Matt would amount to anything because the only thing I knew was girls. I didn't know the first thing about raising boys."

"But you met Carl, who you married, and he turned out to be a good stepfather," I encouraged. "He took me to ballgames and he was a good grandpa to our kids."

"Yes, that's right," Mom nodded. "There were also two other men who were helpful with you boys—two young men. I'm talking about Bill and Neil" (Bill and Neil married my two oldest sisters).

I turned to Linda because I wanted to say something I knew she'd get a big kick out of. "Linda, did you know your husband Bill was the guy who gave me 'The Talk' when I was a kid?"

"'The Talk?'" Mom repeated, curiously.

"The Birds and the Bees, Mom," Linda explained. "No, Tom, I didn't know that."

"Yep, he took me out to Opal's Café. The only problem was I was a teenager and already knew everything he was explaining to me. But it was a thoughtful gesture anyway," I said with a chuckle.

"And I remember a kid who was picking on you because you didn't have a dad," Mom recalled. "It was Neil who said, 'I'll take care of him.' And I guess he did since I never heard another word about it," Mom smiled sweetly.

"Do you remember when I joined the Air Force?" I inquired.

"Certainly I remember," Mom answered. "You sprang it on us so suddenly. I didn't have much to say about it. I just had to accept it."

"You guys took me to a Cardinals game the night before I shipped out," I said as I thought back on that time in my life. "Then we went to the hotel the Air Force was using to put us up. It was a real dump, remember? I remember you were crying on the sidewalk as the bus came to take us to the recruitment center. We got our physicals and were sent on our way."

Mom sat quietly, so I pressed on.

"I know another reason you were crying," I said, with a slight smirk on my face. "You would never let me get a crew cut, remember? You liked my long curly locks and when the Air Force got ahold of me and shaved my head, you just lost it and cried like a baby."

She didn't really seem to want to be reminded of times I made her cry, so I shifted gears. I was reminded of another time in life so I asked Mom about it. "Do you remember when I told you that I felt called into ministry?"

"Well," she said, "I do remember that you gave me a very long lecture about it, and all I could think of to say was, 'You don't need to talk to me, you need to talk to your wife!'"

"And she was behind me 100 percent," I interrupted. I was on a roll, so I pressed on. "Do you remember the first time you heard me preach?"

"No," was all she said in reply.

Linda and I were both shocked by her honest response. But soon all three of us were laughing about Mom's bluntness. She never sugarcoated anything. So much for her being impressed by my preaching style.

"Well, we all were blessed to be a part of this Zobrist clan," I said, quickly changing the subject. "Can you help me, Linda—exactly how many Zobrists are in our family?"

"Let's break it down by the five siblings, and we'll include spouses, kids, kids' spouses, and grandkids," she began. "I am the oldest and there are 20 of us. Two years later Kathy came along and there are 28 of them. Five years later, Emily was born and she now has 21 in her family. Tom, you came 3½ years later and there are 20 in your family too, right?"

I nodded.

"Matt was born 6½ years after you and he has five. And then there's mom, so if you add them all up…"

"It totals out to 95," I said, double-checking my math. "That's a big family."

"It certainly is," said Mom in full agreement.

"Mom, what word or words come to mind when you think of each of us five kids?" I asked. "Let's start with Linda, since she's the oldest."

Mom thought for a moment and then whispered, "I couldn't live without her." I smiled at Linda as she blushed just a bit.

"How about Kathy?" I pressed on.

"Helpful," Mom answered. "An organized servant who is uncomplicated."

"Emily?"

"Efficient," was her one word reply.

"How about me?" I continued.

"Dependable," she said.

"And Matthew?"

"He's my baby," she answered softly. "I wasn't a very happy person when he came along, but he brought hope into my life." For another moment she was lost in thought and I let her have her thoughts to herself.

"Well I sure can recall when I was in trouble with you, Mom," Linda volunteered, changing the subject a bit.

"How did you know?" I asked.

"If I came home from school and found a note written to me in red ink, I knew I was in for it," Linda explained. "Usually it was for something like a messy room. It used to drive Mom crazy."

"I would have been so ashamed to bring anyone into that room," Mom added, suddenly back into the conversation.

"Everyone's room looked like that," Linda said, attempting to use peer pressure as a way to explain behavior from decades before.

"Yet ironically most of us kids are now meticulous and it's all due to you, Mom," I offered.

"You were a feisty one, Linda," Mom recalled, still focused on her daughter. "When you were twelve I remember telling you, 'I can't wait to see you with a twelve-year-old!'"

The three of us got a good chuckle out of that line, but once again Mom was thoughtfully reflective.

"I don't know what I'd do without any of you kids," Mom repeated softly one more time.

From there, the conversation moved to a different rhythm. Rather than Linda and me posing questions to Mom, it just kind of went into a free-form sharing of random thoughts and ideas about the Zobrist family:

Linda: Mom was a faithful wife and mother. She taught me all about faithfulness. We always had a clean house, clean clothes and good meals to eat.

Mom: My job was to stay at home.

Tom: I remember when I told you that I was going to marry a woman who would stay at home like you, Mom. I remember you said, "Well good luck with that in this day and age!" We were raised in a home where you stayed and didn't leave.

Mom: We didn't even say the word "divorce." I guess I was pretty strict in some ways.

Linda: Coming to know the Lord has helped us all immensely. You obey your parents so that you can learn how to obey God.

Tom: I remember the year Dad died—1967. He died in October. But you know what? That following Christmas just a few months later was the most memorable one I've ever had. Our brother-in-law's dad owned a Western Auto store and that Christmas we had plenty of Christmas presents—all from Western Auto. It was amazing.

Linda: What Zobrists do best in crisis is come as close together as possible.

Tom: Your husband, Bill is the driver of that closeness.

Mom: Yes, that's right. Bill is the rock.

Linda: I have a sweet memory of when you met the Lord, Tom. Bill and I had been praying for you for a long time. I remember you came up to Chicago, where we were living at the time, just to tell us about your newfound faith.

Tom: And then Matt got saved about ten years later in 1986. Before he met the Lord he was living in a room above us and he could end up being pretty loud and rowdy with his friends up there at all hours of the night. One night I had enough and I marched up the stairs dressed in only my underwear to go tell him off. There I was in my tighty whities telling them to keep quiet and to stop cussing because I've got young kids downstairs. Not necessarily my proudest moment, and Matt has certainly come a long way, hasn't he?

Linda: Amen. God is faithful. He is good. We trust Him.

Tom: It's what this book is all about---look what God can do. It's the story of His gracious work in the lives of this dear group we call Zobrists.

As I left the facility that morning, I saw a beautiful 8 x 10 color photograph handsomely framed, placed conspicuously on a shelf in the main lobby. It was a picture of Mom, holding a copy of the newspaper announcing that the Cubs had won the World Series after all those years. My mom is a rock star. No one else had their picture in the lobby. Just saying...

CHAPTER TWELVE:

A PARENT'S PERSPECTIVE

It was amazing to me that once the Cubs won the World Series and Ben was named the Most Valuable Player, people began reaching out to me with requests to come and speak at their meetings. A wide array of opportunities began presenting themselves, and I accepted several of them. The following few chapters showcase some of the presentations I made to a variety of groups: A Fellowship of Christian Athletes meeting, a Mayor's Prayer Breakfast, and a group of financial planners. You'll see some material you're already familiar with, but I hope these chapters will give you some additional insight into how my life has changed in the past year.

It became clear to me right away that because Ben was such a strong Christian, unashamed of his faith and straightforward in his testimony, people concluded that it must be the result of perfect parenting; which was far from what really happened. We did some things right in raising our kids, but we fell short in some areas as well.

So when the local arm of the Fellowship of Christian Athletes invited me to address their meeting in March of 2017, I accepted the invitation because I wanted to set the record straight.

Their local leader, Cole, introduced me and I started in on my speech, which I entitled "A Parent's Perspective."

"Cole sent me a list of past speakers; Bobby Jones, J Leman, Dennis Swanberg, Kurt Warner, Trent Dilfer, Ben Zobrist, Colt McCoy, Andy Studebaker, Tim Tebow, Andy Benes, Roger Powell, and me. I feel like I'm playing a game of 'Which of these doesn't belong?' But seriously, I would like to thank Cole for the opportunity to share "A Parent's Perspective" and encourage you in your walk with Christ, especially as it pertains to sports and giving our young people some guidance.

While shut up in prison during some of the darkest days in Israel's history, Jeremiah heard from the Lord God,

> "Call to Me, and I will answer you, and show you great and mighty things, which you do not know." –Jeremiah 33:3

Jesus said in a familiar passage,

> "But seek first the kingdom of God and His righteousness, and all these things shall be added to you." –Matthew 6:33

Cindi and I believed that if we tried to apply these principles (and many others from the Scriptures), that God would do "great and mighty things" in our lives and in the lives of our kids. Our main priority was always that our kids understand the Gospel: That Jesus died and rose again for their sins and that by placing their faith in Him, they can have eternal life. I'm thankful they have all done that and are seeking to serve the Lord with their lives. That should be every Christian parent's priority, especially over sports.

I have a picture in my office of Ben catching a fly ball during the 2008 World Series, and Ben wrote on the picture, "From the back yard to the World Series; look what God can do!" For these few minutes, let me share how God worked in our lives as God led Ben from Eureka High to MVP of the World Series. I want you to know that God blessed us in spite of our efforts at times, not because of them. It is His work for His glory!

Along with their trusting in Jesus for salvation, there were some other principles that we reinforced that would need to be applied during our kids' decision making opportunities. We wanted them to seek God's will, not their own. James 1:5 promises that if we lack wisdom, God grants it. He doesn't want us to wander aimlessly. He will guide us if we seek His will. We wanted our kids to be mentally tough; to not be quitters when life gets hard; to pray through difficulties and trust God in trials. We wanted them to work hard, knowing that God's will requires our cooperation.

> Proverbs 13:4 says that, "The soul of the lazy man desires and has nothing; but the soul of the diligent shall be made rich."

Ben's first year at Olivet, his scholarship required that he clean the freshmen dorm bathrooms.

We wanted them to be consistent and courageous, never fearing to take chances or failure in the process. All of these would be needed in what lie ahead in life, and it happened sooner than we thought for Ben.

As Ben matured and was becoming more independent, it was through the efforts of FCA at Eureka High School, a program that Bob Gold was instrumental in getting going, that Ben started to learn "Doing Sports God's Way." He didn't always have the best example in me, since many times I focused on the results rather than the process of faithfulness. I'm sure my negative attitude at times contributed to him having an unhealthy emphasis on sports during high school, which he readily admits. Fortunately, he had some good coaches that emphasized teamwork, unselfishness, hard work, and commitment. When we do that, the results will take care of themselves. In unspoken and sometimes spoken ways, he was learning to do sports God's way. That would carry him through his college and pro career.

Looking back, I can see that God was working the whole time, transitioning Ben and us gently from the safety of our home and little church and little community to being able to survive and thrive in the world of professional baseball. Ben had learned through that transition that God had to be number one and that baseball was an avenue to serving Him, not an end in itself. The night before he left for Albany New York, and his rookie league assignment with the Tri-City Valley Cats, as he lay in bed, I sat on the edge and we prayed together. He told me not to worry; that he was going to play in the big leagues and he was going to be a missionary to the people he had contact with there. "I'll be like any other missionary, but I won't need financial support. But I do need prayer." God had prepared us to let him go where we never would have four years before.

We had one more transition to make; perhaps the hardest one of all; from the Cardinals to the Cubs. We needed nine years at Tampa Bay and one year split between Oakland and Kansas City to prepare us for this move. The year before he was a free agent, he asked me at Christmas what I would think if he went to the Cubs. With Joe Maddon just going there, he thought they might try to sign him. I was shocked to realize that I would maybe like him playing for the Cubs! Their family would be closer to home and the Cubs had a young and exciting team. I found myself at the end of that process actually praying that God would work out the details, since it was something he really wanted. Long story short, when he told us the news that he was signing with the Cubs, we were, ironically, in the parking lot of the St. Louis Airport; we did the walk-off dance; Ben and Jules and Cindi and me. I experienced what I already knew, that when we desire God's will, he changes our hearts to want what He wants for us. When we pray, God changes us!

I was talking to a reporter after the World Series this year, and a light bulb went on in my head. What we prayed for all along for Ben was happening tenfold. We wanted him to have a ministry for Jesus Christ; we wanted him to serve the Lord; we wanted to him to be a Godly testimony in all He did; and although he is far from perfect, God has answered and is answering those prayers.

But here's the light bulb moment: I almost stopped it! I had this narrow vision of what could happen and God had this huge plan that I could never imagine. I realized that sometimes what we want is small in comparison to what God can do if we let Him.

> If I get out of God's way, He can do "great and mighty things, which you do not know." –Jeremiah 33:3

Ben has had the opportunity to talk to thousands of people. Please pray for his testimony! And I have the chance to share our testimony for you and have my name added to that list. (I call it the Cub effect.) I learned that God can do this in my kids' lives, my grandkids lives, people at church, anyone over whom I might have influence! I need to stay out His way! From the backyard to World Series! Look what God can do! Our God is amazing!

If you are a young person here or a parent or a coach who is a believer, I encourage you to seek God's will for yourself, your family, and your team. It might not be what you envisioned, but it might be what gives God the biggest platform and the most glory! As I heard my own son say once, something like this:

> "Man's glory is fleeting, but God's glory is forever!"

I have five great kids that were all influenced by FCA, where they enjoyed fellowship and worship with like-minded peers and where they learned about leadership, service, and teamwork. I would like to thank Cole and his staff and all the volunteer coaches, teachers, parents, and financial supporters that make it possible for our kids to learn to "do sports God's way."

Julianna singing
the National
Anthem at
Wrigley Field

CHAPTER THIRTEEN:

SIX STOCKS TO INVEST IN

It was a beautiful morning in June and I was up early, in the car, heading to Evanston, Illinois, to make a presentation to a group of financial planners known as Investment Planners Incorporated. One of their group had heard me make a presentation to his church and asked if I would do the same during their annual meeting. Since I always customize my presentations to fit the needs of the audience, I tweaked it a bit and agreed to speak to their group.

I arrived at the Hilton Orrington at 11 AM, thirty minutes before the presentation was scheduled to begin. I was directed to the Ballroom, where there were banners hanging on all the walls with the IPI logo, along with the theme of the annual meeting, "Sharpen Your Game." Chicago Cubs hats were generously featured on table displays throughout the room.

Once I was introduced, I stepped to the lectern while holding an object in my hand. "This is a ball from the 2016 World Series. It's signed by my son, Ben Zobrist, and I'd like to present it to your President, David Koshinski. Thank you for having me here today to share my heart with you."

The group applauded as David accepted my gift to him. At that point I placed my notes in front of me and began my prepared remarks.

Thank you for the opportunity to be here. I really appreciate financial planners and how they can help people manage their assets; prepare for the future. We kind of do the same thing. You help people prepare to have a good life here and now and I, as a pastor, help them to prepare for the then and there, if you know what I mean. I do have a financial planner, but I don't think he is very good. I stopped by his office one day and asked if he could check my balance and he tried to push me over.

Before I begin, I want to say that I have four other kids that are MVPs (Most Valuable People) that have equal value to our more famous son and whom I pray will always find God's will for them as has Ben.

It is interesting how much thought we put into planning for college and retirement and how little we think about eternity. People are the only things that last for eternity.

Ben's dream was never to play professional baseball. He really wanted to play Bradley basketball. His mother's and my dream for him and for all of our kids was that they serve the Lord in some way.

I have had several parents ask me what I thought they should be focusing on to help their kids excel in baseball. We focused on six things for all of our kids. To relate to the world you are used to, let's call them Six Stocks To Invest In. These are the areas that Cindi and I emphasized to our kids. We are definitely not experts in raising kids and give God all the credit for any good in them or us.

1. INVESTING IN SPIRITUALITY

Matthew 6:33 says, "But seek first the kingdom of God and His righteousness, and all these things shall be added to you."

Our main focus was to make sure that they understood the Gospel of Jesus Christ and could have enough information in their little brains that God could use to draw them to Himself, and they could trust in Jesus to save them. I went to Bible College with three kids already in the house, so Ben was immersed in the Word from his earliest of years.

Ben was three years old the night he got saved while sitting in his bed. We saw immediate changes in his behavior. As an example, in our family we believed in strict discipline. If you misbehaved, you went to your bedroom where you would wait for me. Once I arrived, you would 'assume the position,' meaning you bent over so I could give you a swat on your bottom. I can remember before Ben was saved that I would go into his bedroom and he would stubbornly just sit on the bed, refusing to bend over. As a matter of fact, I can remember one time waiting 45 minutes for him to submit to the discipline. Being born again made a huge difference in the life of that little boy. He became much more sensitive to others and much more obedient to his mom and me.

2. INVESTING IN GOD'S WILL

James 1:5 says, "If any of you lacks wisdom, let him ask of God, who gives to all liberally and without reproach, and it will be given to him."

Many books have been written on this subject. My definition is that God's will is a combination (in this order) of God's plans, our prayers, a commitment to His Word, and our desires. When God knows that you want to pursue what He wants for you, He puts the desire in your heart and the skills in your body and mind. He did this for Ben. As a matter of fact, he let Ben know this before his parents.

We thought all along that once he graduated from high school, Ben would be going off to Bible College in order to study for the ministry. But he became aware of a tryout that led him to a scholarship offer to play baseball at Olivet Nazarene University. All by himself, as a Christian young man, he needed to discern God's will for his life. Bible College or baseball? When he made his decision, I remember him saying he would be submissive to our desires, but he felt he wasn't done with baseball yet. I admit, it was different than I thought it was going to be, but God used it in a powerful way. I remember the night before he left for Albany for his first minor league assignment, I sat on his bed and we prayed. Ben considered himself a missionary going to reach people in baseball. The Lord has used him. His testimony has reached far beyond that. He has had the opportunity to talk to players, fans, reporters,

families, executives, congressmen, senators, and even presidents!
Two in one month.

> I often think of Proverbs 22:29,
> "Do you see a man who excels in his work? He will stand before
> kings; He will not stand before unknown men."

Ben has had many opportunities, and I pray that he will always maintain
his testimony. Even though my vision for Ben's life was important, I had
to come to the point of admitting that God had something bigger and
better. God's will is always best, big or small in our eyes. To Him, His
plans for us are always big! It was essential for me to get out of the way
of God for Ben to fulfill God's vision for him. I need to do this with all
of my kids. Get out of the way so that God can lead them.

3. INVESTING IN MENTAL TOUGHNESS

> Philippians 4:6-7 says, "Be anxious for nothing, but in everything
> by prayer and supplication, with thanksgiving, let your requests
> be made known to God; 7 and the peace of God, which
> surpasses all understanding, will guard your hearts and minds
> through Christ Jesus."

It bothers me that some people view Christians as weak whiners. Some
of the toughest people I know are strong Christians. I pushed Ben to
be tough when he was younger, to a fault. I focused on the results more
than the process. I never let him quit on anything. If he was going to do
something, he was going to do it right. Never quit; never say die. Always
try to be stronger mentally. There were many post-game lectures in the
car or at home. It was well intentioned, but sinful at times. (When I see
parents sometimes doing the same things, it makes me cringe and I feel
again the conviction of my own mistakes.) Ben, as a kid, maybe didn't
like being pushed as much as I did, but today he sees the benefits of the
good parts of that now as an adult. He told me he wants his son Zion to
learn to push through things that he is afraid of or that are hard. If you
want to be good at what you are doing, you have to push through what
hurts or is scary. One of Ben's coaches when he was young said that he
had the heart of a lion. Ben was not the biggest kid, but he never backed
away from anything and he would find a way to win or be successful.

We all remember the pressure on Ben when he came to bat in the last game of the World Series. My wife Cindi was literally crying during his at-bat. But I reminded her that those are the opportunities you want. And sure enough, Ben hit a double and the rest is history. You will not always be successful on a human level, but that's not what is most important. My prayer during that at-bat was that Ben would glorify God in success or failure. Either way, God's love and our love for him would be the same.

4. INVESTING IN HARD WORK

Proverbs 13:4 says, "The soul of a lazy man desires, and has nothing; But the soul of the diligent shall be made rich."

I stressed this, but this was born in Ben. He was always willing to work harder and longer than any coach expected.

I can still remember one time putting Ben to bed as a child, only to discover that he would get out of bed and begin doing sit-ups after bedtime. He was like that in all his athletic endeavors. He would sprint around the track when he was supposed to be jogging. Since he was recruited as a pitcher at Olivet, the coaches wouldn't let him field ground balls during practice. I remember one particular occasion when we waited for him at Olivet so he could take ground balls after a double header for an hour because he wanted to play shortstop. He would drag me out to pitch to him for hours. He is an extremely hard worker, in the cage and all over the field. I've gotten slower and he much stronger. He has increased and I have decreased, if you know what I mean.

5. INVESTING IN CONSISTENCY

Matthew 25:21 says, "His lord said to him, 'Well done, good and faithful servant; you were faithful over a few things, I will make you ruler over many things. Enter into the joy of your lord.'"

Being a man of your word is so important. Ben told me as we discussed this once that my own willingness to do the dirty work and serve others and our family set an example for him. Men, it's important to live what you teach. If you are a hypocrite, it will be spotted quickly by your children. You must be consistent in your Bible reading, prayer, church attendance, service, language, the way you treat their mom, etc. They must see Jesus as your example and then they can follow you and eventually the Lord. When you fail, that's okay. Be willing to say you're sorry when necessary and begin again. God still loves you.

6. INVESTING IN COURAGE

> Joshua 1:9 says, "Have I not commanded you? Be strong and of good courage; do not be afraid, nor be dismayed, for the LORD your God is with you wherever you go."

If you are in God's will, you don't have to be afraid of doing anything or saying anything. God will give you the wisdom you need. Don't be afraid of trying new things. I tried to teach our kids that you don't need to be afraid of anyone or anything. Don't be afraid to try new things.

When Ben was in middle school, he set the high-jump record as a 7th grader just because the coach asked him one time to try something different. A change of pace. He went to State in high jump both years. That record has fallen, but his record running the mile still stands.

Don't be afraid to get hurt. This is something that has stuck with Ben that I have long forgotten. The occasion Ben remembers took place during warm-ups at a little league tournament. He was coming off an injury—a bruised kidney. It was a painful injury and took some time to fully heal. I could tell by looking at him that he was being timid, holding back, not going for it completely. I pulled him aside and told him that he couldn't play the game in fear. I told him he was okay and could play the game as he had before. I told him he couldn't be afraid of getting hurt in his life. We cannot live our lives in fear. If we are doing what God wants us to do, nothing can touch us if God doesn't want it to. And if He does, it ultimately is for our best, even though that is hard to understand.

CONCLUSION: Those are the six stocks you'll never be sorry you invested in: A spiritual relationship with Jesus, following God's will, mental toughness, hard work, consistency, and courage will make anyone an MVP. It helps us all to practice them and encourage others to do the same.

CHAPTER FOURTEEN:

COMPELLING LEADERSHIP

Among the many and varied topics I've been asked to address as a result of my newfound fame as the father of Ben Zobrist, one of the most fascinating was an invitation from the City of Washington, Illinois, to speak to their annual Mayor's Prayer Breakfast on the topic of Leadership. As I prepared my remarks, it became clear to me that it wasn't just about leadership, but about leadership that is engaging, contagious, and exciting. So, what follows is the presentation I gave, which I titled "Compelling Leadership."

I'm sorry to those of you that thought Ben was going to be here. My wife found out this morning he wasn't coming and she didn't even want to come. Seriously, I want to thank Mayor Manier for the opportunity to be here and share some thoughts on leadership.

When Joe Maddon went to Chicago, Ben thought it might be possible that the Cubs would try to sign him. After winning with Kansas City last year, where else could you go? I mean the challenge of trying to win after 108 years; that's something that the Cubs had that no other team could offer. They also offered leadership. Ben had been with Maddon for nine years in Tampa and Joe's leadership is what made Ben a super utility player valuable beyond his abilities. If you know much about Joe, he has one rule: Run hard to first base—he calls it "Respect 90." If you doubted his ability to lead and motivate, look no further than this last year, when he led the Cubs, with huge expectations, to a championship. How does he do that? Compelling leadership.

Exactly what is compelling leadership? Although we could look to the Cubs' Tom Rickets or Theo Epstein or Jed Hoyer or Joe Maddon, I would rather look at a Biblical example and see what brought him success. Nehemiah was a good example. I have preached through this book twice in my ministry and find many traits of good leaders. You don't even have to be a believer in Christ to benefit from most of these. This is not an exhaustive list, but I have eleven listed here.

1. COMPELLING LEADERS ARE CARING

4 So it was, when I heard these words, that I sat down and wept, and mourned for many days; I was fasting and praying before the God of heaven. —Nehemiah 1:4

They care about something outside of themselves. Nehemiah had it pretty good as the King's Cupbearer, but he also knew of what was being missed by the nation of Israel being out of the land. The best athletes are more concerned about the team than they are themselves. The best leaders in the community have to care about more than their own careers.

2. COMPELLING LEADERS ARE WILLING TO CONFESS SIN—OR ADMIT WHEN THEY ARE WRONG

5 And I said: "I pray, Lord God of heaven, O great and awesome God, You who keep Your covenant and mercy with those who love You and observe Your commandments, 6 please let Your ear be attentive and Your eyes open, that You may hear the prayer of Your servant which I pray before You now, day and night, for the children of Israel Your servants, and confess the sins of the children of Israel which we have sinned against You. Both my father's house and I have sinned. —Nehemiah 1:5-6

Nehemiah doesn't blame-shift the plight of the nation on his forefathers and all the mistakes that they made. He takes accountability and is willing to do what it takes to make amends with God by confessing; agreeing that what has happened cannot continue and needs to be changed. There has been a changeover of the Cubs that has taken place in the last five years to get to the point where they could be successful. They couldn't keep doing business the same way. They had to admit that it wasn't working and begin to do what did work.

3. COMPELLING LEADERS ARE COURAGEOUS

And it came to pass in the month of Nisan, in the twentieth year of King Artaxerxes, when wine was before him, that I took the wine and gave it to the king. Now I had never been sad in his presence before. 2 Therefore the king said to me, "Why is your face sad, since you are not sick? This is nothing but sorrow of heart."

So I became dreadfully afraid, 3 and said to the king, "May the king live forever! Why should my face not be sad, when the city, the place of my fathers' tombs, lies waste, and its gates are burned with fire?"

4 Then the king said to me, "What do you request?"

So I prayed to the God of heaven. 5 And I said to the king, "If it pleases the king, and if your servant has found favor in your sight, I ask that you send me to Judah, to the city of my fathers' tombs, that I may rebuild it."

*6 Then the king said to me (the queen also sitting beside him), "How long will your journey be? And when will you return?"
So it pleased the king to send me; and I set him a time.*

7 Furthermore I said to the king, "If it pleases the king, let letters be given to me for the governors of the region beyond the River, [a] that they must permit me to pass through till I come to Judah,
—Nehemiah 2:1-7

Nehemiah left his comfort zone and ventured into the danger zone. The king could have had him executed for such boldness. He did not do this without much prayer! Compelling leaders are willing to take chances as long as they are not violating God's Word. Think about Joe Maddon hitting Dan Johnson in Game 162 back in 2011. Dan hadn't had a great year, but it worked out. This year in Game Seven, how many of you Cub fans questioned some moves? It worked out. It doesn't always, but Joe has the courage to make moves that are unorthodox, but according to the rules. We can also be unorthodox, but we have to play according to God's rules.

4. COMPELLING LEADERS ARE CONFIDENT IN GOD

> *So I answered them, and said to them, "The God of heaven Himself will prosper us; therefore we His servants will arise and build, but you have no heritage or right or memorial in Jerusalem."*
> *—Nehemiah 2:20*

He knew he could do anything God wanted him to. He couldn't do anything he wanted to do. There is a difference. When we are in God's will, He gives us every resource, every minute, every skill that is necessary to fulfill it. Believing in God to work through us is much more powerful than believing in what I can do. When Ben was batting in the 10th inning of World Series Game Seven, I didn't say, "Come on Ben, you can do it." I prayed that God would help Ben to glorify Him no matter what. God chose to bless him with a double. But I needed to be willing to accept whatever God allowed. We prepare, we work, but we trust God for the results. Paul mentioned in 1 Corinthians 3 in relation to evangelism that "I planted, Apollos watered, but God gave the increase." Compelling leaders are confident in God.

5. COMPELLING LEADERS CAN COORDINATE PEOPLE

Take a few minutes and read all of Nehemiah chapter 3. It names those that were involved in the wall's construction and what they were responsible for. He knew where to put each group so that they could be successful. Joe Maddon is a master of putting players in positions to succeed. From pitching matchups to defensive positioning, he wants the players to be successful. If they are, so will be the team. And so the Israelites were successful.

6. COMPELLING LEADERS HAVE CONTINGENCY PLANS

> *And all of them conspired together to come and attack Jerusalem
> and create confusion. 9 Nevertheless we made our prayer to our God,
> and because of them we set a watch against them day and night.*
>
> *Every one of the builders had his sword girded at his side as he built.
> And the one who sounded the trumpet was beside me.*
> *—Nehemiah 4:8-9, 18*

There were those who threatened the Jews as they built. They trusted
God to protect them, but they were ready if they had to fight. One of
the reasons the Cubs were successful this past season was their depth.
If someone went down, there was another to fill the gap. Compelling
leaders are prepared for the unexpected trial and are ready when
it comes.

7. COMPELLING LEADERS CONFRONT SIN

> *And I became very angry when I heard their outcry and these words.
> 7 After serious thought, I rebuked the nobles and rulers, and said to
> them, "Each of you is exacting usury from his brother." So I called a
> great assembly against them.*
>
> *And it grieved me bitterly; therefore I threw all the household
> goods of Tobiah out of the room.*
>
> *So I contended with them and cursed them, struck some of them
> and pulled out their hair, and made them swear by God, saying,
> "You shall not give your daughters as wives to their sons, nor take
> their daughters for your sons or yourselves.*
> *—Nehemiah 5:6-7; 13:8; 25*

Nehemiah had to deal with various issues that violated God's laws;
from charging interest of Israelite brethren, which violated the Law
of God, housing one of their enemies in a room that was reserved for
the tithes to the priests, to intermarriage. He met each challenge with
confrontation. He didn't want the nation to commit the same sins that
led to the captivity. Joe Maddon is known for being pretty loose in his
management style, but if you loaf to first base, you may find yourself
on the bench and maybe without a job. Compelling leaders have well

defined expectations and then they confront issues in a Christ-like way when they come up.

8. COMPELLING LEADERS ARE CHARITABLE

Now that which was prepared daily was one ox and six choice sheep. Also fowl were prepared for me, and once every ten days an abundance of all kinds of wine. Yet in spite of this I did not demand the governor's provisions, because the bondage was heavy on this people. ¹⁹ *Remember me, my God, for good, according to all that I have done for this people. —Nehemiah 5:18-19*

Nehemiah knew the financial condition of the people and so he did not demand what he deserved. Rather, he bore the financial burden himself. Major league baseball players make a lot of money, but they also donate a lot of money and much is required and expected. The same is true of leaders. You will be asked to make donations, attend fundraisers, and a variety of other activities. That is part of compelling leadership.

9. COMPELLING LEADERS ARE CAUTIOUS AND DISCERNING

Then I sent to him, saying, "No such things as you say are being done, but you invent them in your own heart."

And I said, "Should such a man as I flee? And who is there such as I who would go into the temple to save his life? I will not go in!" ¹² *Then I perceived that God had not sent him at all, but that he pronounced this prophecy against me because Tobiah and Sanballat had hired him.* ¹³ *For this reason he was hired, that I should be afraid and act that way and sin, so that they might have cause for an evil report, that they might reproach me.*

¹⁴ *My God, remember Tobiah and Sanballat, according to these their works, and the prophetess Noadiah and the rest of the prophets who would have made me afraid. —Nehemiah 6:8; 11-14*

As long as we are not doing what is wrong, we have no reason to fear. God will protect us if He wants us protected. We should be in the business of being a God-pleaser, not a people-pleaser. Do you remember Game Six of the League Championship against the Dodgers? Kyle

Hendricks had pitched, gave up two hits, had faced the minimum, and Maddon came out of the dugout to pull him, under a chorus of 42,000 boos. The Cubs were about to win the National League pennant, and the fans were booing the manager. Joe was not trying to please God I don't think, but he certainly wasn't trying to please the fans. He was trying to win and part of that was being cautious and discerning. Compelling leaders do that. They use care in decisions that they make, if they have time to.

10. COMPELLING LEADERS ARE COMMITTED TO THE WORD

In chapter 8, Ezra reads from the Law, for the first time for most in his audience. This was their new standard. Theo Epstein set in place the Cubs plan five years ago. We have heard much about that plan in recent days. They followed the plan even though it meant they had to lose for a time. Compelling Christian leaders stay committed to God's Word even though it may mean short-term losses; maybe even long-term losses. They have a priority system that places obedience to God above all else.

11. COMPELLING LEADERS ARE COMMITTED TO WORSHIP

The other thanksgiving choir went the opposite way, and I was behind them with half of the people on the wall, going past the Tower of the Ovens as far as the Broad Wall, –Nehemiah 12:38

This is the celebration of the wall and what God had done. The Cubs celebration was a parade of five million adoring fans. Crying, reaching out, screaming, praising, it was all at once exuberant, scary, and sad. And I had a little bit of guilt as I had never suffered as a Cub fan, was at every game, and now was in their World Championship parade. But by God's grace and a generous son that wanted us to be a part with him and his family, it happened. If you're a Christian, I trust you are active in a place of worship. It helps you to stay grounded and gives you a place to serve.

Thank you for allowing me to be part of this celebration today. By God's grace, I trust we all go forward as compelling leaders in our homes, workplaces and community.

"The Lord bless you and keep you; the Lord make His face shine upon you, and be gracious to you; the Lord lift up His countenance upon you, and give you peace. —Numbers 6:24-26

So that's a look at some of the presentations I've made as a result of the opportunities I've been presented in this last year. As we bring the book to a close, I want to finish it up with one of the happiest occasions I've experienced as a result of being Ben Zobrist's dad.

CHAPTER FIFTEEN:

A GAME OF CATCH WITH MY SON

It was Ben Zobrist Bobble Head Night.

Thursday, June 8, 2017, was a picture-perfect day at Wrigley Field. With our youngest son, Noah, and his wife, Courtney, Cindi and I arrived around 2 PM even though it was a 7:10 start, because there were lots of added activities to the normal festivities of the game.

The sponsor for the Bobble Head night was Olivet Nazarene University, the school that first offered Ben the scholarship to attend there and play baseball. Dr. John Bowling, the President of the University, was serving as Master of Ceremonies for a gathering of a few special friends of the University. The specific locale at Wrigley was a lovely little dining area with a wall of clear glass facing the ball field and the words 'Fannie May Bleacher Sweet' painted on the opposite brick wall. We were located just outside the outfield wall in center field of Wrigley. We helped ourselves to warm nachos, fresh-baked cookies and sweet fruit flowing freely from the serving tables.

It was time for the brief program to begin. Dr. Bowling said a few words, followed by Dr. Ryan Spittal from the University. Then it was Allan Kimberly, the Managing Director of the Marquis Sports and Talent Agency. All were good speakers, but the whole room was distracted. Players, both from the Cubs and from the visiting Colorado Rockies, were beginning to warm up outside on the field, so it was difficult to stay focused on a presenter. Everyone seemed to be waiting for a particular player to appear. Before long it happened.

"Here comes Ben now," I alerted the rest of my family, quietly pointing to the tall, slender figure moving toward the outfield along the third base line. Wearing his Cubs jersey (number 18), blue jeans and his trusty pair of PF Flyer shoes, in a moment he was gone from the field and standing in the back of Fannie May's. I felt sorry for Allan Kimberly. Not a soul was paying any attention to the words he was saying.

Dr. Bowling introduced Ben, who strode toward the front of the room right past Cindi and me, but not before giving us both a big hug. He was handed the microphone and began by saying, "Those are my parents," pointing to the two of us. "I don't just hug random people." The crowd smiled and immediately it was clear that he had won the crowd over with just ten words. They were hanging on his every move.

Of course I had heard Ben share his story of how he got to Olivet Nazarene a hundred times before, but I was struck anew as he mentioned the key phrase, "Stay open to God's will for your life." He explained how that was the theme of the church camp he attended right before visiting ONU. He had made plans to attend Calvary Bible College in the fall and yet this visit would change everything.

Dr. Bowling interjected, "We noticed immediately when Ben began at our school that when he gets in, he gets all the way in." And then he turned and looked at us and added, "That says a lot about his family."

The audience was invited to ask Ben questions for another fifteen minutes and he adroitly handled issues ranging from Joe Maddon's managerial style, especially with a utility player like Ben (Joe tells Ben to bring 'lots of different gloves' to Spring Training!), to contrasting the fans in Tampa Bay (loyal fans but a small crowd), Oakland (Not a good time for us—Jules was pregnant and sick, I was injured and it felt way out there), Kansas City (Only there for three months and they were already in first place before I arrived!), and Chicago (a great fan base).

The crowd cheered for Ben as he thanked everyone for being there and made his exit for the dugout—but not before posing for countless pictures, endless autographs of balls, gloves, jerseys, and programs, all with kind patience with each and every fan.

Dr. Bowling invited Cindi and me to the front to share a bit of our perspective concerning the day's events and we were pleased to recount the story of Ben signing with the Cubs as seen through the eyes of a couple of St. Louis Cardinals' fans. Everyone got a big kick out of that story.

We followed the time with Ben with a brief tour of Wrigley Field, held mostly in the right-field bleachers so we could listen to the tour guide while watching the Cubs take batting practice. How fun to watch three young children in our group all walk away with a souvenir baseball hit solidly to the bleachers by a few Cubs sluggers.

Before too long we ended up in another Cubs venue at Wrigley that served as our dining hall for the evening. Endless rows of steam tables offered up a buffet of everything from juicy prime rib to hot grilled sausage to honey-fried chicken to a wide variety of fresh salads and vegetables topped off with some of the best carrot cake on the planet. (I heard about the carrot cake from others—you know I don't eat dessert!)

As delicious as the food was, I picked at it a bit because I knew what was coming up next in the evening's festivities and I was just a slight bit nervous. Actually all of us in the Olivet group knew it...

...I was going to throw out the first pitch for tonight's ball game.

What made this incredible honor even more amazing is that it was going to be a total and complete surprise to Ben. He had no idea it was going to happen. He knew he was to come out and catch the first pitch, but he was assuming the pitch would be thrown by Dr. Bowling or some other administrator from the University. He was in for quite a surprise.

I had been invited only a week before, which was probably for the best, since it meant I had only a week to be concerned about the whole thing. Uppermost in my mind was this recurring gut-twisting thought: I don't want to bounce it and embarrass Ben.

So to ensure I was at my best, I enlisted the help of all of my sons. That week, back home in Eureka, I would play catch with my son Pete, in order to stay loose and work on my arm strength. When we got to Wrigley that Thursday afternoon, thanks to one of the ushers at the ballpark that knew us, I was escorted to a field outside the stadium where I could warm up with my son Noah. And then, of course, Ben caught my pitch in the stadium. I loved it that all my sons were part of the special occasion.

I played catch with Pete.

I played catch with Noah.

I would play catch with Ben.

Soon it was time for us to assemble. I was already dressed in my 'uniform' for the evening—my Cubs Father's Day jersey with ZOBRIST 18 on the back, a dark Olivet Nazarene University ball cap, jeans, and my running shoes. And don't forget my baseball glove—the one I had since the time I was a ball player in high school. I couldn't help but think of the history at Wrigley, the legends that have played on that field, the fact that my dad had taken me to games there over 50 years before. He has been in Heaven since I was nine and I wondered if he knew what I was doing now. The emotions of the moment were deep and strong.

The Cubs personnel ushered me onto the field just to the third base side of home plate. Cindi was with me, along with Noah and Courtney. Just a few moments later, who should appear but all of Ben's family: Julianna with Zion, Kruse, and Blaise in tow.

Noah couldn't resist taking on the role of sportscaster and soon he had his arm around me saying, "Welcome folks! This is tonight's interview with Tom Zobrist, father of Ben Zobrist, who is throwing out the first pitch for the first time in his life." He paused and smiled at me as he said, "And if you throw it over Ben's head, what do you say is going to happen?"

"He's probably going to make me go chase it," I admitted with a bit of a sheepish smirk on my face. That's what I would have made him do.

It was finally time for Ben to come out onto the field from the dugout. "Ladies and Gentleman," the Public Address Announcer beckoned, "At this time kindly direct your attention to the pitcher's mound for this evening's ceremonial first pitch and welcome a guest of Olivet Nazarene, Ben's dad, Tom Zobrist!"

As this introduction was being made, Ben was hustling out of the dugout, still unaware of what was going to happen. Finally he was at a place where he could look at what was assembled behind home plate—his family. I will never forget the expression on his face, especially when he realized it was his old dad who was going to be playing catch with him. He pointed his finger at me and erupted into a huge smile.

He came over and hugged me and said, "How did you get this gig?"

"They asked me!" I exclaimed. "Can you believe it?"

"Oh, that is awesome," he responded. "Congrats!"

"Dude," I answered, "I got my glove—so if it's a bad pitch throw it back to me." He laughed, then couldn't help having a little fun at my expense. As I turned to run out to the pitcher's mound, he whispered loud enough for me to hear, "I'll bet you're really nervous, right? Thousands of people are watching." I turned and watched that lovable boyish grin spread across his face.

Once I got to the pitcher's mound, it all went pretty quickly. I wound up, took my aim and hurled my one and only chance at greatness.

It was more than I could have asked for.

The pitch made it all the way to Ben's glove.

And it was a strike! Ben threw out his right arm just like an umpire!

Thank You, Lord.

Ben and I met midway and once again he embraced me. "That was awesome," he kept saying to me. "Congrats!"

"You didn't know at all?" I kept asking.

"I had no idea," he professed. "They said it was somebody from Olivet."

"Well, we're going to take some pictures. The family is here," I replied.

And then he delivered a line that stopped me in my tracks.

"It's just like old times, only switched around."

My mind was flooded with thoughts that went back as far as this handsome young man being just a baby of eighteen months and me sitting with him in our living room shouting, "Throw me the ball, Ben! Come on, Son, throw me the ball!" And then I would throw it back by aiming for his little glove.

Playing catch with your son has become one of the ultimate metaphors for the bonding between a boy and his dad. And I sure know why. "It's just like old times, only switched around."

We gathered the family together for some special photographs on the ball field and I have to admit, I was feeling good. I felt even better when my sweet little five-year-old granddaughter Kruse came up to me and offered this critique with a smile and a hug: "Grandpa, that was a really good throw!"

Look what God can do!

ACKNOWLEDGMENTS

I first need to acknowledge my Lord and Savior Jesus. He is what gives my life meaning. Where would I be without Him? This book is about His work!

My wife Cindi has been my companion for 40 years. We married young and literally grew up physically and spiritually together. Her courageous witness to me in the halls of Morton High made me contemplate my spiritual life and eventually put my faith in Christ. She has encouraged me through all of life, made our home, and helps me accomplish all God has given me to do. Her input and encouragement—and searching for old pictures—have been invaluable in this project. No doubt our marriage has been a "Look what God can do" experience.

My brother-in-law Bill Morton's encouragement, vision, and support have brought us to this point. He helped me see that God can encourage others with what he is doing in our lives. He also connected me with Bill Butterworth.

My sister Linda Morton, for being an encourager through this project and being a part of my conversation with Mom.

My mom, Shirley Brenkman: Thanks for taking me back in time and talking about dad and life and family and baseball. I love you and appreciate you more than you will ever know.

Aunt Marilyn Donahue: Thanks for allowing us to invade your space and work on the book. Your hospitality was a blessing to us and the environment at the Garlands was perfect for reflecting and writing.

Uncle Noah Zobrist: I know you like to watch the Cubs alone, so I appreciate the opportunity to watch with you and share that experience. I've never been able to watch my son with my dad, but you make it feel like he is there.

My church of 29 years, Liberty Bible Church: Your support and love for our family over the years have left an indelible mark on us all. My service to our Savior and you as your pastor is my greatest privilege. The elders' encouragement through this project has been a blessing.

All my children, their spouses, and their children: Jessica and Robert Reeves, their boys Judson and Wesley Thomas (I had to throw in that middle name!); Ben and Julianna who gave us Zion, Kruse, and Blaise; Serena and Michael Grimm and their children, Lucy, Dylan, and Rex; Pete and his fiancée Anna Lofquist; and finally Noah and his bride, Courtney Zobrist. I have learned so much from all of you—and whether you know it or not, our life experience contributed greatly to this book.

My son, Ben Zobrist: Thanks for taking time in your busy life to read this and write the Foreword. Who better to write it? You have seen the best and worst I have to offer and you still love me. You said it best, "Look what God can do!"

ACKNOWLEDGMENTS

Bill Butterworth's skill in writing and our developing friendship
have been a real blessing. His sense of humor and joy were
an encouragement as I thought back to all that God had done
in my life.

Versa Press and Steve Kennel: Thanks for the advice and the tour
of your facility. Your workers do a wonderful job. Look what God
has done through your family these 80 years!

Jeff Domagalski from Olivet: Thanks for calling me about the
first-pitch opportunity. Your willingness to help and encourage
others is a gift.

Les Lofquist, your encouragement and editing skills helped get this
project ready for the printer.

Converse Marketing: Thank you Amy, Becky, Ted, and Erik; your
availability, talent, and willingness to meet our schedule was
nothing short of a "Look what God can do experience!"